TO CANTERBURY WITH LOVE

To Canterbury with Love

GAVIN REID

KINGSWAY PUBLICATIONS
EASTBOURNE

First published 2002

ISBN 1 84291 066 3

Published by
KINGSWAY COMMUNICATIONS LTD
Lottbridge Drove, Eastbourne BN23 6NT, England.
Email: books@kingsway.co.uk

Book design and production for the publishers by
Bookprint Creative Services, P.O. Box 827, BN21 3YJ, England.
Printed in Great Britain.

For
Colin Reid
pastor, preacher, counsellor and big brother,
not forgetting Jo, who kept him going,
and
for all my friends in
the Diocese of Canterbury

Contents

Introduction

So there I was, sitting within range of the high altar in Canterbury Cathedral on a hot summer's day in 1997. On one side of me sat Cardinal Hume, on the other the former Archbishop of Canterbury Lord Coggan, the most under-rated archbishop of the modern era. Across the cathedral I could see another former archbishop, Robert Runcie, and in the centre, on the throne of St Augustine, sat the incumbent archbishop, George Carey.

We were celebrating the fourteen-hundredth anniversary of the landing of St Augustine on the Thanet coast to re-evangelize the south of England. The Prince of Wales was in the congregation and the organist was going over the top. Every line he played in his voluntary seemed to be trying to outdo the grandeur of the line before. I was beginning to wonder how much longer he could do this before the organ blew a gasket, or whatever overworked organs blow. And there was something else that I was wondering. *I was wondering what on earth Gavin Reid was doing in such a place, on such an occasion, in such robes and in such company.*

There I was, however, and directly across from me was my

fellow suffragan bishop in the Diocese of Canterbury, Richard Llewellin. Together it was our responsibility to 'run' the diocese on behalf of the incredibly busy archbishop. And together, I dare to believe, we had developed an episcopal partnership that was unique in the Church of England. That does not mean it was better, just different and surprisingly great fun.

From the time when my parents had me baptized, somewhat irregularly, in a Carlisle parish, through my later experience of a Church of England primary school, through an amazing Sunday school, a vibrant youth fellowship, theological college and two curacies, through work in religious publishing and then eighteen years of consultative work in evangelism among Church of England parishes, through nearly fifteen years in the General Synod and finally eight years as a bishop, the Church of England has been my constant companion. I have been blessed by it, annoyed by it, angry with it, proud of it, honoured by it and, on a couple of occasions, humiliated by it. The truth is that I love it.

To have ended up as a bishop in the Diocese of Canterbury still makes me want to pinch myself and ask if it was all a dream. I never expected to be a bishop and I did nothing right to put me in the frame. Running Billy Graham missions is hardly what one expects to find in an episcopal candidate's CV.

One of the more dubious privileges of being a bishop is the daily receipt of all the day's press cuttings relating to the affairs of the churches. It usually makes depressing reading. Our newspaper editors seem to feel they have a calling to present the Church as a quarrelsome, declining, out-of-touch, disorganized and irrelevant body of people. Sometimes on reading the cuttings I have slipped into depression, sometimes

I have felt very angry. Sometimes I have wept. I simply do not recognize the Church of England that I read about in the newspapers.

Which brings me to this book. I want to write about the Church of England that I have known for over half a century, as both man and boy. I want to talk about the good things I have found, but I also want to talk about the real difficulties it is facing and the challenges and dilemmas that confront it. I believe the Church of England as we have known it is fighting for its life, and I am not sure whether it can – or, indeed, should – survive in its present form.

These are very difficult times, but the simplistic analyses of so many commentators do not go to the heart of the difficulties. In this book I want to suggest what some of our problems really are and what we need to do about them. There are proper criticisms that should be made, but they come best from those who love the Church.

I worked for eight years as a colleague of Archbishop George Carey. I believe he was a good archbishop and I respect him enormously. I think it is important to make clear, however, that the views in this book were not discussed with him and I do not expect that he would want to agree with some of the things I say.

This will be a critique in places, but it comes from someone who owes just about everything to the Church of England and who longs to see it find new ways of being the people's Church in a nation that desperately needs to be reintegrated and re-focused under the influence of the greatest story ever told, the story of Jesus Christ.

So this is what I want to say *to Canterbury with love*.

Gavin Reid

1

Starting with a Splash

I hope it was a lovely summer's day. It ought to have been. It was the first day of August, and the year was 1934. It was the day when I first met the Church of England and I have a certificate to prove it.

The man who officiated at my baptism was a certain Reverend C. R. Burnett, Vicar of St John's Church, Upperby, on the outskirts of Carlisle. The interesting thing was that neither of my parents lived in his parish. Indeed, my family did not even live within the jurisdiction of the Church of England. We were based in Scotland at the time. Yet it seems that the vicar did not turn a hair. There is no record that he asked any questions or saw my parents beforehand to ascertain the strength of their beliefs.

Perhaps the reason why he was so unbothered related to the fact that my father was the son of his lay reader who was also headmaster of his church school. Perhaps, and I incline to this view, there was nothing too unusual about these circumstances. The Church of England in the 1930s was pretty laid back about its candidates for baptism. The majority of children born in the country were presented at the font. England was, after all, a 'Christian country'. The Church of England was part of the wallpaper. It may have been taken for granted, but it was generally recognized as a 'good thing'. It was not a golden age in terms of numbers. Sunday congregations were not particularly remarkable, but Christmas, Easter and Harvest pulled the people in. Folk religion was strong and recognizably Christian.

Reid family baptisms at Upperby were capable of being somewhat out of the ordinary. When my father was taken to be baptized the family decided, and I believe it was actually on the way to the church, that the name they had earlier entered on his birth certificate would have to be changed. He had been registered as William Arthur Reid, but when someone pointed out that this gave him the initials W.A.R. and that a terrible conflict was then ensuing in South Africa, his forenames were reversed at the font itself. He was called Arthur from that day onwards and it led to innumerable legal hiccups for the rest of his life.

So England in the 1930s assumed that Christianity, or certainly 'church', was part of the landscape and the clergy usually worked on the assumption that people believed even if they did not practise their religion to any great extent. The jargon word for the Church's strategy is 'inclusive'. People had (as they still have) a right to the baptism of their children, not because they clocked in at church or swore affidavits about their beliefs, but simply because they lived within the parish boundaries. *People were to be counted in unless they obviously counted themselves out.*

By the time I was ordained in 1960, things were beginning to look different. The men who had come back from the battlefields of the Second World War were changed people. The working classes had provided the regiments who had preserved democracy for the United Kingdom. They had seen their friends lost in the same cause. They knew they had a stake in the nation. They helped to vote in a Labour government in 1945 and their vision of a future Britain was one where privilege and set ways had to change.

Perhaps there was also something deeper. They had seen terrible things and many felt that they had done terrible things. Talk of a loving God who was supposed to be 'almighty' took a lot more believing. Again, a significant proportion of the nation's males had been lost in action. Increasingly the congregations of our churches became dominated by women. When growing boys were old enough they could be like their fathers and opt out – if they were ever in. As we shall see in the next chapter, the Sunday schools of the nation still seemed to account for half the child population in the mid-1950s, but the slide was beginning and by 1960 those numbers were in sharp decline.

The drift away from church allegiance was well set by 1960 and the ten years that followed saw it move from a drift to a drive. And it was literally 'a drive'. The increasing overall prosperity of the late 1950s and the early 1960s meant that more and more people became car owners. Sunday became a day for the family drive. I remember, in my first curacy, that one of the pressures felt by teenage Sunday school teachers was whether they should give up their Sunday responsibilities to be with their parents on the weekly outing, or whether they should stand firm to their Christian obligations and risk being branded as disloyal to the family.

The people of England began to feel more distant from the Church, and the Church began to feel more distant from the people. One of the movements within the Church at that time was known as the 'Parish and People' movement.

Essentially it was a renewal movement. It sought to remind the Church of England that it was about the people of God before it was about the people of England. It sought to sharpen a congregation's sense of identity as a worshipping community. It emphasized the central place of the Communion service or Eucharist. One of the catchphrases of the day was 'the Lord's service for the Lord's people on the Lord's day'.

Thus at the very time when fewer children were being brought to the font after birth, the Church was beginning to ask questions about their suitability. Were parents aware of the significance of baptism – or 'christening' as it was more commonly called? Did they have any real intention of encouraging their children to come to Sunday school and later to public worship? Would those parents be setting an example and coming with their children?

In my first parish in east London we visited parents and tried to explain what baptism meant and how it was not a private matter but about becoming a member of the Church. The parish next door, St Barnabas, Manor Park, was led by a remarkable priest called Nigel Porter, much involved in 'Parish and People'. Those wishing to have their babies 'done' in his parish found that they were required to attend a series of four preparation evenings.

Nigel told me of one of his parishioners who was so outraged at this requirement that he hawked his baby round every other parish in the area looking for a better deal. Alas, from his point of view, none of the other clergy would play ball. He was told that they could not baptize someone from outside their boundaries and that he should go to his own parish priest. Not to be outdone, the angry parent wrote to the bishop. He received a curt letter saying that he should not have gone to the other parishes and that he should abide by the procedures of his own church. This was the last straw. Clutching the bishop's letter in his hand, he stormed round to Nigel's vicarage and snarled, 'If you ask me, it's all a filthy plot to get people to go to church!' And he was absolutely right.

The big difference between the Church in the 1930s and the Church of more recent years is that the edges between congregation and community have become increasingly sharp and more clearly defined. The years leading up to 1960 were years when the Church of England was comfortable about nominal Christianity. While one can never generalize, a large number of the clergy saw nominal Christianity as something positive that could be 'worked with'. The prime-time Sunday service was usually Matins, a service of the word rather than of the sacrament. People attended on equal terms as listeners in the pews. For many, of course, it was far more than listening, but there was no public sign required to indicate the depth of their concern. No one in the pews was required to reveal his or her commitment. The liturgical renewal after the Second World War (within which Parish and People was one of several players) began to change the culture of the nation's Church. The move to make the Eucharist the prime-time service had the effect of heightening the congregation's sense of being a community in debt to Christ, but it also had an effect on those who had been able to hide their non-commitment in Matins. With the call to come forward to receive the bread and wine, people were put on the spot. The Church was beginning to move from inclusiveness to exclusiveness. *It was beginning to count people out unless they very obviously counted themselves in.*

Thirty years after my curacy days in East Ham I found myself serving as the Bishop of Maidstone. Bishops get letters – lots of letters. Among these letters there can be letters of complaint about the supposed shortcomings of particular

clergy in the diocese. I am glad to say that I did not receive very
many such letters. I think my clerical colleagues within the
Diocese of Canterbury were pretty conscientious as well as
sensitive. I do remember, however, receiving letters of complaint about the baptism policy of a certain very conscientious priest. The thrust of the letters was that he made things
almost impossible for parents who were not regular attenders
to have their children baptized.

Now this sort of complaint puts a bishop in a very difficult
position. The last thing he wants to do is to undermine the
parish priest. On the other hand, a bishop – even if no one else
bothers about it – has to uphold canon law when the chips are
down. With a heavy heart I summoned (well, politely invited)
the priest in question to come and see me to discuss the com-
plaints I was receiving about him.

I remember being anxious to avoid any sense of confrontation. I took the trouble to brew some really nice coffee, only
to find that he was fasting that day. (If there is a book on *How
to Make Your Bishop Feel Inadequate* he must have been
reading it!)

Before he arrived I had done my homework and mugged up
the particular canons affecting baptism. When he arrived I
found he was carrying his own copy of the canon law, ready
to do battle. It was the only time in my eight years as a bishop
that I found myself debating the meaning of a canon with a
parish priest. Most of the time we have better things to do!

I pointed to those parts of the canon that made it clear that
he could not refuse or unduly delay the baptism of one of his
parishioners. He pointed to that part of the canon which mentioned the importance of due preparation. We ended up in a
dead heat with little gained from the exercise. What we both
had to agree, however, was that a caring minister could not be

casual about creating settings where people make promises to God that they either do not understand, or have no intention of keeping.

In many ways, baptizing the infants of non-attenders is the moment of truth for a Church which understands itself to be 'there' to serve all the people of the country. Sixty years ago when I was christened, parish priests had good grounds to be fairly relaxed. They had reasonable expectations that the parents would show up in church on some festival or other and certainly that the children would become Sunday school pupils in later years. Today things are unrecognizably different.

When we hear talk of 'disestablishment', the real crunch is not whether there are bishops in the House of Lords. It is whether there is any longer some meaning and sense in the idea of a Church with a national chaplaincy role – 'there' for the people of England, no matter how much they believe or otherwise. To have a commitment to serve the people of a nation is a noble thing. There has to be, however, a higher commitment if a church is to be truly Christian. That commitment, of course, is to Christ himself.

Saying this, however, does not simplify the matter. Jesus Christ was and is no inflexible set of principles, even if sets of principles can be adduced from reflecting upon his life and teaching. Jesus Christ was on earth as a person, and it is as a person that we must remember him and celebrate his cause. St Paul called his followers to be imitators of Jesus.

If, as I believe, Jesus was uniquely 'of' God in a sense that the word 'Son' is as near as we can get to the truth, then he came into a world that was united in non-belief about him. He welcomed any and every person who was open to receive his ministry and learn from him. It follows that any church which seeks to be an embodiment of the personality and character of Christ needs to clutch at every straw of openness in those who cross its path. And, yes, perhaps this can look like lowering standards, but Jesus was frequently accused of lowering standards and consorting with the wrong sort of people. And, yes again, living this way means that people will 'use' clergy and congregations.

Again, if we are true to the Bible's picture of God we have to believe that his purposes are being worked out through all that happens. This is called the doctrine of providence. It is a hard doctrine to hold when one contemplates some terrible disaster or massacre, but a doctrine of providence does not mean that God approves of all that happens. What it does mean, however, is that there can be good outworkings even from bad happenings, and that the eye of faith needs to be looking for this. It has always seemed to me that when someone comes to a vicarage door to request baptism for their child, in a society where God gets constantly forgotten, the minister must start from the assumption that God is behind the occurrence.

I am glad that a certain Reverend C. R. Burnett baptized me all those years ago. What might have happened if he had refused? Obviously I do not know the answer to such a hypothetical question, but I do know what has happened in some cases where clergy today have bolted (or appeared to bolt) the baptismal door. I remember confirming someone from a parish where a previous vicar had taken a strong stand against 'indiscriminate baptisms'. He told me that he had refused to go to church again as a result of his encounter with that vicar. Fortunately, a new priest several years later had managed to repair the damage and the man himself was brought to clearer faith and genuine commitment.

The conclusion I have drawn over the years is that when a church tries to deal with public ignorance about the importance of baptism, it falls foul of the very thing it has rightly identified as the problem. The degree of ignorance in many people means that they cannot understand the theology that is being put to them. All they can see is that they are being rejected or that they are not considered 'good enough'. Thus at the very time when openness to the Church is being demonstrated – no matter how much confusion accompanies it – the response of those who represent Christ is seen to be rejection.

Such a view does not remove the obligation on churches to try to help people understand what they are doing and, indeed, promising. Canon law, as my fasting priest pointed out, recognizes the need for instruction. We need, however, to think carefully about what we do by way of 'instruction'. One of my clerical heroes, long retired, a certain Reverend Tony Waite, used to invite groups of parents who wanted baptism for their children to meet with him on two occasions before the service. The setting for such gatherings was social rather than educational and he always tried to have parents from the regular congregation present. He believed that there was very little he could get across in terms of actual teaching. What he hoped for was that the members of his congregation who were present would be good advertisements for the cause, and that friendships might emerge. The actual learning would come later. His strategy proved to be remarkably effective.

What Tony Waite was doing was recognizing that understanding is not everything and it is rarely where you begin in a relationship. If Christians really believe that God is alive and longing for people to discover his presence, then what the Christian minister should be about is making encounters possible. Understanding will follow. And if we are to believe that in some sense a congregation is a dwelling place for the Spirit of God, then encounter with the people of the congregation can be a stepping stone on the way to encounter with God.

It is here that one of the big differences between baptisms in the 1930s and baptisms in the years since 1960 reveals itself. I was almost certainly taken to church in mid-afternoon, to a service in an almost empty building, where the family and its friends made up the congregation. Perhaps there might have been several families together. The regular congregation, however, would not have been present.

The Book of Common Prayer envisaged something very different. In the introduction to the baptism service we find these words: 'Baptism should not be administered but upon Sundays and other Holy-days, when the most number of people come together: as well for that the Congregation there present may testify the receiving of them that be newly baptized into the number of Christ's Church.'

It is to the credit of Parish and People and others involved in the liturgical renewal in the 1950s that a serious attempt was made to deprivatize baptisms and to return to something near what was envisaged in the Prayer Book. Tony Waite, who was much influenced by the renewal, used to have a monthly baptism service incorporated into Morning Prayer. The service would start with the parents and baptismal parties in church but with the babies being minded in the church hall. At a magical moment in the service, well after the sermon, a hymn would be sung and the babies were carried into the church, in a joyous procession, and given to their parents. The promises and the baptisms followed immediately, with the whole congregation present and enjoying the proceedings. The service was brought to a close as soon as possible after the baptisms.

The intention behind this approach was that parents would see that baptism was about belonging. It was also hoped that through the relaxed preparations and the feel of the service itself, the parents would actually *experience* belonging. In the 1960s and 70s it was to prove remarkably effective.

Things may well have become harder since Tony Waite's time, but churches have a habit of making things more difficult than they need to be. I have seen churches trying to do all baptisms in the weekly Parish Communion service with the children being present from the start. I have seen the regular congregation (often dominated by the elderly) finding it difficult to cope with the noise and restlessness, while the baptismal parties looked bewildered at what was taking place. When the time came for people to go forward to receive the elements, their 'outsiderishness' became painfully apparent.

The happiest solution, I have always thought, is when baptisms take place in an informal Family Service. Such services can have a far more welcoming feel. They can also bring the baptismal families into contact with others of their generation in a worship setting marked by a sense of enjoyment, even fun. There is the real chance that fringe baptismal families might feel drawn to come again to similar services. My guess is that churches which hold such services have the best record in holding on to those fringe families that request baptism.

There are those who feel that the Church of England's canonical procedures concerning the baptism of infants are no longer credible, if indeed they ever were. They would argue that the whole business is mocking a holy God and allowing his Church to bring Christianity into disrepute. Some of those who feel this way have networked together under the name of Baptismal Integrity (formerly the Movement for the Reform of Infant Baptism). They have strong arguments to put

forward and I feel that, with every year that passes, those arguments become stronger as the level of understanding behind
many who seek baptism for their children becomes weaker.
What we need to see clearly, however, is that the implications
of the 'reform' of infant baptism in the English context inevitably carry over into the reform of the established nature of
the Church of England. I feel that it is no accident that my
friend Bishop Colin Buchanan is both president of Baptismal
Integrity and the strongest campaigner among the bishops for
disestablishment.

In 1950, 67 per cent of all live births in England were baptized in the parish churches of the country. In the years since
then there has been a steady decline, until we come to 1998,
when only 21 per cent of all children born in England were
brought to an Anglican font. Such a decline is sad to contem-
plate, but it raises an interesting question. If it is no longer the
norm, and if it is no longer fashionable, why do one fifth of
the nation's young parents still seek to have their children
christened? In a strange way it makes me feel increasingly
determined to keep the door open. If the first disciples of
Jesus 'left all and followed him' without a clue as to what he
was all about but because they felt a pull to do so, is it so dis-
honouring to Christ to welcome those who feel they want
their babies 'done'?

What is highlighted in this current dilemma is that the
Church of England has got to learn how to work with openness rather than understanding. For years, thanks to the
strength of cultural Christianity in Britain, the Church in its
ministry could make connections with people that opened up
discussion about God relatively easily. Far more people
prayed than ever came to church, and the notion of the God
to whom their prayers were addressed was a recognizably

Christian one. Things are different now, but if God has indeed made us in his image, there will always be what the Quakers call 'that of God in everyone'. The task of the Church of England in today's society is very different from what it was on that August afternoon in 1934 when a tiny boy named Gavin Hunter Reid was baptized in the name of the Father and the Son and the Holy Ghost. But that boy remains grateful that a few rules were bent so that it could take place.

2

'From a Child . . .'

Her name was Miss Seeley and the year was 1943. I cannot remember what she looked like. I was nine years old at the time and feeling very strange.

My family had moved to south London from our home in Greenock in Scotland. My father had moved with a change of job a year earlier. The Greenock house had been sold within months, and my mother and I had lived out of suitcases and with relatives for the best part of a year.

Now we had found a home and my parents had to find a school for me. This was not difficult. We found that we were living about 200 yards from a Church of England primary school. I was duly enrolled and nervously began to attend. That is where Miss Seeley comes in. She was the so-called 'parish worker'. They did not ordain women in those days. Women who felt a call to serve the Church would receive sound theological training, only to be deployed as something like ecclesiastical charladies. Perhaps I am being a touch unkind about the Church of those days, but I would never wish to be unkind to Miss Seeley because something she said to me changed my life.

I had only been a pupil for about a day or so when Miss Seeley arrived for one of her regular visits. As I was the new boy in school, we were introduced. Her first words to me were the ones that changed my life. She said, 'You must come to Pathfinders!' She was referring to a Sunday school for children of my age. The next Sunday, having nothing better to do, I set out from my new home and walked to the small hall near the parish church. It is worth noting that there was a war on and the walk involved crossing busy roads. I had responsible parents, but it never occurred to them that I might be in any danger. Children lived far freer lives in those days.

Pathfinders proved to be something very special. It was run by a courteous, elderly man called Mr Dick who was assisted by his adult son, Alex. The programme consisted of hymns and choruses sung boisterously, with brief prayers and two stories. The first would be a Bible story and the second was 'an everyday story' which in some way underlined the Bible teaching. The whole thing was run in a way that broke all the rules. There was no breaking up into smaller classes with craft work thrown in. The only craft work I can remember was when children folded up their hymn sheets and launched paper aeroplanes all over the place. And there were plenty of children, close to a hundred.

Mr Dick and his son were good storytellers, but that was not their main gift. Old Mr Dick was far more than someone who talked about Jesus – he was someone who reflected him. He was gracious and kindly and obviously loved being among boys and girls of our age. His concern for us went beyond the Sunday sessions. My wife, who was also a member of Pathfinders, remembers a time when she had to go into a London hospital for an eye operation. When she emerged from the anaesthetic, the first person to come to her bedside was old Mr Dick with a bunch of flowers and a reassuring smile.

It was only some years later that I realized that old Mr Dick was the chairman and chief executive of a large industrial concern. He was far more than a quaint elderly man, and in fact he may not have been as elderly as we nine-year-olds imagined. More than that, he financed all that happened. Within two or three years of my joining Pathfinders there had to be two sittings to get everyone in, with a larger hall being used in the afternoons and a morning session in the original hall. Some 150–200 children a week were sitting at the feet of old Mr Dick and his son, learning about the Jesus he so obviously loved. He met all the expenses of those sessions, paid for a Christmas party for every child (with a new shilling in their pockets as they went home), and financed the annual trip to Chessington Zoo for a party of children and helpers numbering nearly 250. Buses, entrance fees, circus seats and teas were all paid for. Not surprisingly, Sunday school numbers always increased in the few weeks before the summer outing. I once heard the old man say, 'Isn't it wonderful how attendances go up every year at this time!' I cannot believe that he could not see why this was the case.

In my later teens I was drafted in as one of a small number of people invited to share the up-front role alongside the two men. I have often said that standing in front of 150 children, armed only with a microphone, taught me more about public speaking than anything I learned at theological college, not least the importance of storytelling.

The time came when old Mr Dick retired from his company. His son, who was also on the board, did not succeed him. He took the opportunity to leave the company and travel to Tanganyika (as Tanzania was then called) and to teach at a missionary school in Dodoma. The old man went with him and it was not long before he was once again doing what he loved best, telling children about Jesus. His fame spread far and wide, and an African bishop once said, 'If you send a letter to "Mr Dick, Tanganyika" it will get to him!' When he died, I am told that he was buried not alongside the expats but alongside the Africans he had come to love and to serve.

And so the years passed, as they do, until we come to an October day in Canterbury in 1992 when I was robing up to be consecrated Bishop of Maidstone. In the room with me were about ten other bishops who had come to support me and to take part in my consecration. Suddenly the door burst open and a large, smiling black bishop from Tanzania walked in. He had not been invited, but he was over on business in England and had heard about the consecration. In every sense of the word, he had come to lend a hand. His name was Alpha Francis Mohamed, Bishop of the Rift Valley. He may not have been invited, but he made my day!

I had invited 'young' Mr Dick, Alex, to the service, and when we were all milling around at the reception I found him in warm conversation with the African bishop. I discovered that Alpha had been a scholar at the school where Alex had taught. I found out something else, too. Like me, Alpha had also sat agog at the feet of old Mr Dick. Like me, he had never forgotten the man or the story that he had to tell.

The fact that Alpha Mohamed and I both owed our faith to what happened in our childhood is nothing unusual. When I was working on the 1991 General Synod report *All God's Children?*, I took the opportunity to ask a simple question of every adult group of church members I met. The question went as follows: 'How many of you, as you look back on your lives, would now recognize that you had taken significant steps towards the faith you now have, before you were thirteen years of age?' Everywhere I went, my *ad hoc* survey came up with the same answer. About 65 per cent of those asked – and I asked nearly a thousand people – had taken those steps to faith in their childhood years. Some years later, I spoke to a group of Episcopalians in Alabama and could not resist putting the question to them also. I received the same answer.

In 1992 John Finney published a small but helpful piece of research under the title of *Finding Faith Today* (Bible Society). With a team of helpers, he had studied the conversion stories of over 500 adults who had come to faith within a year or so of the survey. When the report was published, what the press focused on was the fact that very few of the people in the sample had been brought to faith through set-piece evangelistic missions. People came to faith more through relationships than through special efforts. What nobody at the time seemed to identify, however, was something which I feel to be even more significant. In the second chapter Finney writes:

> The importance of early encounters with the church can be seen in the figures for those who had no contact with the church. Only 10% never went to Sunday school or church and another 13% went only occasionally. *Thus 76% of those who became Christians as adults had a reasonably prolonged contact with a church during childhood – this is a good deal higher than the population at large.* (p. 12, my italics)

Finney's research on how adults came to faith makes, in fact, a powerful argument for the value of children's ministry. A 1999 survey conducted in the United States by the Barna Research Group revealed that ministry to children did far more than prepare them for adult commitment. It revealed that American people were many times more likely to begin lifelong believing before they were thirteen years of age than at any other time in their lives. From a sample of over 4,000 people they concluded that if people do not make a commitment to Christ by the age of fourteen, 'the likelihood of ever doing so is slim'. Using the somewhat curious angle of 'the probability of accepting Christ', the Barna findings showed that between five and thirteen years of age a person had a 34 per cent 'probability' of 'accepting Christ' compared with a figure of 4 per cent for those in teenage years, and 6 per cent for those who were nineteen or over.

In his comments on the findings, George Barna wrote, 'The statistics are eye-opening because they show how little evangelistic impact we are having in America upon teenagers and adults.' Such words are all the more remarkable coming from a researcher in the USA, the country of Billy Graham, Campus Crusade for Christ, Evangelism Explosion and many other initiatives designed to reach adults and teenagers.

In 1985 I took part in a consultation with a number of church leaders in north-east England. We had been working together for several years to prepare for and to follow up the great meetings that Billy Graham held in Sunderland the year before. Over 120,000 people had come to hear the American evangelist preaching in a cold, windswept football stadium. Over 11,000 of them had 'got up out of their seats' to indicate a response to his preaching. The question we were asking ourselves, and which was directing our prayers, was simple: where do we go from here? We all knew that churches cannot rely on a continuous diet of special missions. We knew that somehow the excitement and the vision of those great meetings had to translate back into the ongoing life of the churches and parishes. But was there some great priority we were meant to be identifying?

It was during a prayer session that it came to me. I had opened my eyes and my glance settled for a moment on one of the people present. He was a full-time children's evangelist. It was almost like the proverbial shaft of light hitting me. Of course, I thought, the key is ministry and outreach to children. I did not immediately make connections with my own experience. I was thinking (yes, I know I was supposed to be praying) more strategically than nostalgically.

It had long been clear to me that Billy Graham's kind of evangelism was a second-stage evangelism. He needed to build on a previous awareness of the story of Jesus Christ. Preaching evangelists in the classic mould are building on foundations that others have laid and calling their hearers to make a response. Many of those who got up out of their seats, night after night, were doing so because the memory of Christ had been reawakened. They were not turning to Christ so much as *re*turning.

The problem I was seeing with increasing clarity during that prayer meeting was that a far smaller percentage of children in the 1980s were learning about Christ from Christians than had been the case in my day. If the trend continued, then those preaching to adults in future years would be starting from scratch when they ought to have been making connections with what was already there.

Within a few months of that consultation I began to speak about the need for the churches to put more energy into reaching the many children outside our congregations. I began to find, however, that this was not a message that met with much enthusiasm. I think there were a number of reasons for this. The first of these may well have been that I was exposing an area of failure in the churches. None of us likes to be told that we are failing in something, and church people are no exception. People in Christian ministry live, as St Paul did, with the evidence of rejection and failure ever before them. Feelings of disappointment, and even guilt, are never far away. I was trying to inject a sense of urgency, but it may be that I was generating guilt. In 1985, when I started saying these sorts of things, the churches were already on a downward spiral concerning the numbers of children they were reaching and holding.

The second reason for coolness towards my message was that children's work has rarely been taken seriously by church leaders, local or national. So often Sunday school and the like was the preserve of enthusiasts like old Mr Dick, but not something that engaged a great deal of the vicar's attention. My guess is that ministry to children took up very little space on the agenda of the House of Bishops. It certainly never appeared as a serious agenda item in my five years in the House. I had to make myself an irritant in the mission section of the Lambeth Conference of 1998 to get some recognition that children's evangelism was a separate and important issue and could not merely be blurred into talk about 'youth'.

The third reason for the unresponsiveness I met was different. It came from many of those who actually specialized in children's ministry. Many such specialists working in the major denominations were people drawn from the teaching profession. As such, they saw their job as ensuring that the children already in our churches were receiving the best possible Christian education. They did not see their role in evangelistic terms – indeed, many of them had a profound distaste for what they believed to be evangelism. As educators of people at a vulnerable stage in their lives, they saw the dangers of anything that might pressurize or manipulate.

Alongside such fears I suspect that, for many, there was a theological factor. They did not take the concept of 'salvation' seriously, and therefore the urgency to reach children (or anybody, for that matter) was lost on them. Talk of salvation has a built-in logic, and that logic leads to the conclusion that those who are not 'saved' must in some sense be 'damned'. Talk of damnation, not least in the context of work with vulnerable young children, was abhorrent to most denominational children's work specialists, and I can sympathize with their fears. There can be no doubt that there have been some pretty horrific cases of emotional abuse of children by well-meaning Christian workers, all in the name of 'salvation'. I have personally never believed it right to offload the damnation agenda on children.

So it was that I found I was not scratching where the Church felt it was itching. Nor was this coolness confined to those who were out of sympathy with my basically conservative theology. Many children's workers who shared my convictions about the need to reach unchurched children with the story of Jesus nevertheless believed that such children should only be reached in the context of their families. By the 1980s there was a widely held view that the old children's Sunday school was a flawed strategy. It singled children out and kept them at arm's length from the fellowship of the congregation. It left those children who responded to Christ in the nurture of unsympathetic parents. Its weakness could be seen in the huge fall-off rate that followed the Sunday school years. In other words, the Mr Dicks of this world were seen to be discredited.

Whichever way I looked, whether to theological friend or foe, it seemed to me that my thoughts were out of fashion. The orthodoxy seemed to be that we must reach children within the family unit and in all-age contexts. In today's circumstances, I felt that meant we were condemned to talk only to the children of church members and a few of their friends. People with more experience than I had (or still have) seemed to be resigned to the fact that the scale of outreach of the old Sunday school would never again be realized.

While I recognize that the format of the old Sunday school has to be left behind, I am still convinced that we can find ways to reach very many more children with the gospel than we do at present. If we are to reach them in numbers, however, we have to reach them in their peer groups rather than hoping for families to come together. I also believe that too much is made of the great fall-off after Sunday school. The big question is not whether youngsters (and the adults they later become) stay with us. *The big question is whether we, and the things we taught and shared, stay with them*. Over the years in my own ministry, I have seen adults returning to what they first held as children. That is surely what John Finney's work in *Finding Faith Today* proved. Somewhere inside our heads there is a hard disk with a memory for everything we have experienced, especially if the experience was good. Our task in the churches is to make sure that as many people as possible have good memories associated with the story of Jesus Christ and the people who believe in him.

In 1988 the General Synod of the Church of England was asked to debate a report entitled *Children in the Way*. The report came from the Board of Education and its main thrust was to press the Church to face the fact that children were part of the Church of today rather than the Church of tomorrow. Churches were asked to examine whether their worship was child-friendly, and practical suggestions were made. It was a good report, but when I read it I became aware that it reflected the educational mind-set. It had very little place for ministry to the children presently outside the churches, although it included a section on those who were on the fringe.

I was, at that time, a member of the General Synod, so I put down an amendment. My amendment asked for the Board of Education to join forces with the Board of Mission and look further at the question of bringing the Christian gospel to those children totally outside our ranks. I made sure that the Bishop of London, who was presenting the main report, saw what I wanted to say and I was delighted to hear him commend my amendment in his opening address. The amendment was carried and it was not long before I found myself on a working party preparing a further report. After over two years of discussion, our report came to the Synod in the autumn of 1991. It was called *All God's Children?* and it asked for nothing less than a total change of mind concerning the spiritual plight of the nation's children. The report and its recommendations (which I can now see were too modest) received overwhelming support.

The report stated that the day would never return when large numbers of children would be parked by their parents on Sunday afternoons in the local church hall. There were now far more options for children or families on Sundays. Churches had to put more energy into activities at other times in the week and in very different contexts from 'church' or 'Sunday school'. We had to see ourselves as competitors in a marketplace seeking the interest and attention of today's children.

The report quoted the 1989 English Churches Census finding that 'church attendance' levels for children had fallen more steeply during the 1980s than had been the case for adults. It calculated that only about 15 per cent of the nation's children had any sort of contact with any of the Churches. The report claimed that the world in which our children were growing up was not neutral. While Christianity with its values and its vision impinged less and less on the minds of children, materialism and hedonism were increasingly taking centre stage.

After the first round of press interviews, which were mostly concerned with one paragraph in the report that mentioned Barbie dolls, and after a few desultory presentations to busy diocesan synods, the report sank with little trace. By the year 2000, things had become even more serious. The loss of children to the Churches had again plummeted during the preceding ten years. We are now in danger of turning Christianity into an adults-only phenomenon. About 40 per cent of our churches, across all the denominations, have no children's ministry at all. The Church is surely no different from any other community of people. No children can only mean no future.

At the same time, however, the new Archbishops' Council has identified children's evangelism as one of the priorities for the Church at large. Perhaps the crisis that *All God's Children?* identified in 1991 needed to become a catastrophe before such a slow-moving institution as the Church of England could be expected to respond. At the beginning of 2001, the archbishop created a national post for children's evangelism and invited me to represent him on the appointments committee. It is, perhaps, significant that it needed an initiative from Lambeth Palace to make good a deficiency in the official structures. The children's work of the Board of Education still concentrates its efforts on what we do with the diminishing numbers that we already have, while the Board of Mission still focuses the majority of its efforts on work with adults, who are far less likely to respond to Christ.

I believe that the Church of England is genuinely moving towards a recognition of the importance of children. I believe it is beginning to see the need to reach out beyond the numbers we have to the millions who go through each day without meeting people who believe in Jesus Christ and can share his story attractively. A long history of neglect and uninterest, however, takes a great deal of overturning. One person with the title of Archbishop's Officer for Children's Evangelism, no matter how talented, is hardly likely to turn the tide. For all the changes of concern and priorities at the centre, what we need are more people like Mr Dick. They will, of course, have to work in ways that the old man would never recognize. Almost certainly the centre of gravity will move away from Sundays to midweek evenings and Saturdays. The fast-growing concept of Kidz Klubs, spawned in the back streets of New York, may well point the way forward. Already England has them in some of its big towns and cities, and already many hundreds of children are gathering for their unconventional ways of telling the story. Already churches are taking initiatives in linking with schools to run imaginative after-school clubs, and again are reaching large numbers. For some years holiday clubs have pulled in thousands of children to enjoy their blend of games, crafts and Bible stories.

The cause is not yet lost, but the daunting challenge is that the cause simply has to be won.

* * *

When I stood up to speak in that General Synod debate in 1988, I was not sure how much time I would be given. To meet this problem I drafted two speeches, one for ten minutes and one for five. Quite often in the Synod I would speak from the scantiest of notes, but I knew on that particular occasion I had to have things tightly under control.

Part of the reason for this rests with something I discovered when I first started speaking about the subject of reaching children for Christ. I kept finding that my emotions became almost uncontrollable, and I would choke over a massive lump in my throat. I have often wondered why, and am still not sure. I think, however, that it has something to do with my deep admiration for a courteous old man who used to radiate the love of God as he stood up in front of scores of children and talked about Jesus. And I sometimes think that my whole ministry has been a prolonged 'thank you' to God for that day when a certain Miss Seeley said, 'You must come to Pathfinders!'

3

Charlie's Angels

It was a fairly typical November day. The year was 1995, and my wife Mary and I were driving to Blackheath, a place of many memories. We had not long returned from a trip to South America on behalf of the Archbishop. Mary had caught an unpleasant infection in Argentina and had been confined to her bed immediately on her return. She had only a few days to recover, but she was determined about it. The occasion in Blackheath, where we had grown up, was too important to miss. If representing the Archbishop of Canterbury in Chile and Argentina had been a great honour (and it had been), the invitation to that November gathering in Blackheath was even more significant.

Thus a barely fit Mary and I made our way on a damp and cheerless Saturday afternoon to a hall that was far from plush, to join with scores of people of our own generation, and we did so for one reason only. We were all products of the youth work of a remarkable man, and forty or so years later in life we had come together to pay our tributes to him. An imaginative circular letter had called old friends together, and all of us agreed with the sentiment it contained. If film stars can have great tribute events in their honour, then surely Charlie Cope, youth leader extraordinary, deserved nothing less. From all over the country we came. He was that sort of a man.

Charlie had grown up in Bermondsey, south London. He came from a working-class family and at the age of twelve had been converted at a camp run by the Cambridge University Mission that was based in his area. Called up for military service in the Royal Air Force, he had studied accountancy in what spare time he could find. With the war over, he had continued his studies and, when I first knew him, he was gaining his accountancy qualifications. He was married and had three children. Life must have made many demands on him, and yet the reason I knew Charlie Cope had nothing to do with the world of accountancy. I knew him, at first, as a cheerful and attractive Bible class leader. The group he led, which must have numbered about fifty or so early teenagers, met on Thursday evenings for games and outings and on Sunday afternoons to study the Bible.

Charlie was a strong leader and his group, known as Junior King's Own, grew and brought a very talented group of boys and girls together. Mary and I rarely missed a meeting. As the years progressed, the group grew up together and became the senior group – known, unsurprisingly, as King's Own. Charlie transferred up with us to the senior group and this made even more demands on his time. There were Easter sailing holidays on the Norfolk Broads, with him as 'commodore'. There were summer Saturday afternoon tennis sessions in the local park. There were bank holiday hikes, carol singing round the parish every Christmas, and crazy concert evenings, all on top of a commitment to regular Sunday and midweek meetings.

Charlie was always there. Perhaps he was with us a little too much, but his wife, Irene, was patient and supportive of what he was doing. And all the time his responsibilities at work increased as he moved steadily towards company director status.

Charlie was resourceful. When I was doing my national service in the Royal Air Force, there was an occasion when all leave was going to be cancelled because of an important air officer's inspection. I duly told Charlie that I would not be available that year to serve as his vice commodore on the annual sailing holiday. A short while later I was summoned to the adjutant's office at my RAF station. I wondered what I had done wrong. I arrived at the office with freshly pressed uniform, saluted, and found the adjutant looking very purposeful. 'Ah, Reid,' he said. 'The station commander has just received a letter from a Mr Cope. Apparently you are very important to Mr Cope's plans for running a youth adventure project, and he is asking that you can be granted leave to take part. The commanding officer is pleased you are so public spirited and has agreed to this.'

A few years earlier, Mary had a similar experience when her college term dates ruled out the possibility of sailing with the Easter cruise. She found herself called to see the principal, and learned that a certain Mr Cope had written to say that Mary was indispensable to the smooth running of this very worthy annual youth project. She was excused lectures. I wish I knew how to write letters like that!

Charlie, however, could be firm and brooked no nonsense when standing in front of a Bible class. I shall never forget the October Sunday in 1948 when my disruptiveness in Bible class led to the following rebuke: 'Gavin – out! And don't hang about outside!' I can still remember his words exactly.

They shook the cocky fourteen-year-old who had been trying to impress the girls. I do not consider it to be a co-incidence that a few days later, a much more thoughtful and chastened fourteen-year-old took a clear step of commitment to Christ.

Our meeting in Blackheath on that November afternoon in 1995 was a great time. People who had not seen each other for over thirty years clicked into old friendships as if nothing had happened. Old stories were told. Laughter flowed freely. Speeches were made and presentations given. One thing that became clear was that King's Own had led to many marriages, and almost every one of them had stuck. Another thing that stood out was the number of Charlie's former young people who were in formal Christian ministry, or – just as important – pillars of local churches, and parents who had given a Christian upbringing to scores of children.

Charlie loved it, and Irene looked on bemused and pleased for him. I have often thought about Charlie Cope, just as I have often thought about Mr Dick. For me, they and others like them are the real Church of England. What happens in Synods, and pronouncements from bishops (especially when they appear to be about doubt), are what the press thinks the Church is about. The press is wrong. The real Church of England is about what happens in, and because of, the parish churches, and the most talented clergy imaginable can do very little without the contribution and commitment of the lay members. If we could have found one Charlie Cope for every parish in the Diocese of Canterbury while I was there, we could have transformed it.

Charlie's youth fellowships of the 1940s and 50s were not unique. The years immediately after the war were years when large numbers of adolescents were in our churches, or at least caught up in fringe activities. Apart from the cinema, there were few other attractions. Sunday was a fairly uneventful day. Large numbers of teenagers had come through Sunday school. They knew the story and the stories of Jesus, and had made friends with their peers in church contexts. The media and commerce were not, in those days, polarizing the generations and targeting teenagers as a lucrative market. Public transport was cheap and widespread, allowing youngsters greater mobility than they have today. Rock concerts did not exist, but in London the evangelist Tom Rees filled the Royal Albert Hall fifty times over with young people for memorable rallies. Summer camps and house parties run by Christian organizations were thick on the ground.

Leadership was also in relatively plentiful supply. There were a good many Charlie Copes to be found. Like Charlie, they were mostly themselves the products of attractive and energetic Christian youth work, and they were locked into a tradition and a set of values. There was enough leisure time available to them, and there were far fewer recreational opportunities on offer in society at large. That said, things were changing.

The two pieces of the jigsaw that gave the Charlie Copes such fertile soil to work in, and which gave rise to such people in the first place, were beginning to go. The first of these was the strong role that many churches had in the social life of their surrounding communities. This meant that young people were accessible to them – indeed, large numbers had come through the numerically successful children's activities. The advent of widespread car ownership in the later 1950s changed that and broke the Church's strong bonds with the children of the nation as Sunday schools began to shrink.

The second piece of the jigsaw was that the time pressures felt by adult members of the churches were considerably less than one would find today. In the closing decades of the twentieth century, Britain moved from a full-employment society where most workers (shop-floor and management) could leave their jobs behind when they left the workplace, to one where there was higher unemployment and where those who had jobs were often under pressure to work longer hours. These longer hours and higher pressures were felt more by those with leadership potential than by others. When churches look around their memberships for volunteers today, the constant cry is that people are 'too busy'.

Things were beginning to change even when I was in Charlie's Bible class. In 1945, the Church of England published a challenging report called *Towards the Conversion of England*. The report opened with an analysis of the spiritual situation of the nation, and went on to say some pretty unflattering things about the ability of the clergy and the commitment of the laity. Clearly the authors had not read *How to Win Friends and Influence People*! The section on lay commitment startled me. Here is what it said about the problem of people being too busy:

> The objection, 'I have not the time to give,' is of modern currency. Before the 1914 war the principle (if not universally recognised) largely obtained of every keen communicant undertaking some kind of church work – Sunday School and Bible teaching, district visiting, club and youth-organisation leadership. With the increase of leisure and of opportunities for entertainment, such posts have become more difficult to fill; and the shirking of duty has been greatest among those who have had most leisure to enjoy.

I continue to be amazed that those words were written in 1945. If the number of leisure-time opportunities in the late 1930s and early 40s was weakening the commitment of lay Christians, how much more could it be doing so in today's world, where leisure is a major industry and Sunday is a multi-choice exercise? Is the truth of the matter that church members rate their leisure-time activities higher than the cause of Jesus Christ? Is it fair to look at our church members and talk about a 'shirking of duty'?

A friend of mine wrote to ask if I would come to his area and speak about evangelism. In the course of his letter, he set out some reflections on the lifestyle and culture of the people in the churches where he was working.

> The large majority of younger (i.e. not-retired) Christians are totally caught up in the materialism trap – frenetic activity, usually associated with paying a huge mortgage, and if they have got on top of that, they are caught in the trap anyway. We spend more and more of our time sitting in traffic . . .

The problem of the mega-mortgage is certainly something that Charlie Cope and his generation did not have to face, nor was it something on the minds of those who wrote so critically of lay commitment in *Towards the Conversion of England*. There can be no doubt that this is a factor affecting the availability of time and effort from many of our younger lay members. Many young couples are forced to work long hours simply to pay for the exorbitant prices of houses in many parts of the country. When there are children with both parents working, free time, especially at the weekend, is precious – and there are strong Christian reasons for giving quality time to one's own children as well as to each other as husband and wife.

I would therefore want to make a strong plea for mitigation on the lay commitment issue, but I still feel that a few other considerations also apply. All of us belong to our culture. It is impossible not to be affected by the values and practices of one's own society, and we need to be realistic about the huge influence on all of us of the consumer mentality. While few doctrines are ever preached or articulated, most of us are seduced to some extent by the supermarket mind-set. We are the consumers and choosers and all around us, sitting attractively packaged on the shelves, are the choices we can make.

Thus life today, and especially at the weekend, throws a wide range of attractive options in our direction. The local church, whether it likes it or not, is in competition with Sunday sport (especially for children), recreational shopping, concerts and cinemas, outings in the car (very often to or from relatives) – plus the growing phenomenon affecting so many children: which separated parent should I be with at the weekend? In this sort of world, congregational Christianity has to sell itself in a buyers' market. Some may find this very unpalatable and there are plenty of pious rejoinders to what I am saying, but the truth remains: if our package has little appeal, there will be little take-up.

In saying this, I am not only talking about the possibility of attracting new worshippers. I am talking about keeping the ones we already have! In recent years, our 'regular' worshippers have been expressing their regularity in terms of the number of times they attend each month rather than each week. All this is a far cry from the involvement of people like Charlie Cope, and the effect on the work of the local church is immense. There simply are not the people on the ground to give time to children's and youth work, and those who could do it are hard pressed because of mega-mortgages or distracted and seduced by the consumer mind-set.

It is important to be clear about the nature of the consumer mind-set. This mentality does not only see life as a whole lot of competing choices. It sees the individual as the ultimate chooser. Within this mind-set, and with no sense of rebellion against God entering one's consciousness, Christianity is a choice I make as the main player in life with the right to choose what I want to choose.

There is a further factor that makes things so very different from the days of Charlie Cope. Quite simply, there are far fewer young adults in our congregations than there were fifty years ago. The growing weakness of Christian work among children and young people since 1960 means that there are significantly fewer young adults in our churches, and young adults are the ideal people to lead children's and youth work. The whole thing is a sort of vicious circle. When I was a teenager, Charlie Cope must still have been in his late twenties or early thirties, and the congregation had others of his generation within its ranks. Weakness in youth work inevitably feeds into a paucity of young adults with a Christian commitment. This shows itself in the number of young men and women in training for the ordained ministry. When I was ordained in 1960, I was one of a batch of about thirty candidates and, if I remember rightly, all but one of us were in our twenties. In the late 1990s, the average age of a new deacon was around thirty-eight. The same dynamics feed through into lay ministry. I remember being shown the average age of our Readers in the Canterbury diocese. We had practically no Readers under fifty, and the new entrants in training were overwhelmingly of the same age band as those in service.

If the churches are to see a significant upturn in work

among young people, two things will need to be in place. First, there needs to be a quantum jump forward in the numbers of children who come within the ambit of our congregations and who experience the Christian story being told in ways that attract and convey relevance to their young but worldly-wise lives. Second, there needs to be a greater number of committed Christians, clerical and lay, with quality time to offer. Congregations will also need to understand that the cultural gap between today's young people and the world of the Church is immense and almost unbridgeable. Youth workers will have to live very dangerously. That is why I am increasingly of the mind that youth evangelism can no longer be done from the heart of the congregation. We need people working in extramural settings and using formats that would probably scare our congregations out of their minds.

To put it another way, if we are to evangelize young people today we have to work where they are, and for the vast majority that means well outside church services and fellowships.

As I look back to the days when scores of teenagers who named the name of Jesus looked to Charlie Cope for leadership, I cannot see how present-day young people could be reached and held by the way he and others like him worked. There simply was not the gap between church culture and youth culture that there is now. Indeed, I do not think one could talk meaningfully about any distinctive 'youth culture' in the mid-twentieth century.

Since the 1950s, a number of things have come together that have changed youth evangelism into a cross-cultural activity. The biggest factor is affluence and the fact that young people in an increasingly wealthy society become an important target market. They have disposable income and few responsibilities. Because of this, together with steady technological progress, we have the rise of the pop industry that not only produces product for the youth market but also nurtures a heightened sense of corporate identity. The pop stars are icons and their values are magnetic. They are important not only to the music industry but also to any other industry targeting the youth market. Magazines and clothing aimed at young people are usually tied into pop stars and sports personalities. The advertising that accompanies youth market products also reinforces the values and sense of corporate identity.

Young people's and children's television is again reinforcing the sense of corporate identity and the values and the fashions. And all the time, music dominates. It thumps out from ghetto-blasters and the open windows of youngsters' cars, and it chatters ceaselessly into their ears from personal stereo sets. It is a music that is usually alien to older generations. For many, all this crowds out creative talent and turns young people into consumers. Until the mobile phone came along, it even showed signs of destroying all forms of conversation! This music that dominates our youth culture, however, is performance music rather than participation music. It was nothing unusual for me as a teenager to join with my peers singing cheerful Christian songs and hymns. Such activity would be alien to most of today's unchurched youngsters.

In 1999, the Archbishop of Canterbury challenged each diocese to find and send 100 young people to London for a weekend of activities, starting with a concert in the Royal Albert Hall. I was at that concert, as were most of the bishops. What struck me was that the musical idiom presented by 'Christian bands' was something that could never be envisaged in the majority of our churches. They were working within the musical idioms of the youth culture. The volume was almost painful and the words, to my mature ears, were indecipherable most of the time. That, however, was not the point. The point was that everything was presented so as to create moods rather than to communicate thoughts. The dominant moods were great excitement and something close to physical and emotional abandon. It was as alien to the hymns of Wesley as it was to the worship music of much contemporary Christian song-writing.

While I felt some alarm at the irrationality of all this and found it mind-bending at times, that is not my concern. I am more than willing to acknowledge my age and to recognize that the elderly have always criticized and expressed bewilderment at the antics of the young! My concern is that none of this is within the capacity or tolerance of the average congregation, which has a culture that is still recognizably similar to the one I experienced fifty years ago.

If the churches are to make real inroads with the gospel to the present generation of young people, we will need to look to specialists and structures that sit loose to the regular worshipping congregations. Of course we should never generalize about any generation or group of people. We still have access to a significant number of young people and children, as the archbishop's weekend in 1999 proved. I would not want to suggest that churches abandon what they are doing when they are making some progress. What I am saying is that we need to branch out in new ways, and we need to find a large number of trained and dedicated full-time youth ministers. While there has been little central direction about this, there is clear evidence that what I am saying is being recognized. Full-time, salaried youth workers (some rather amateurish, but many clearly skilled and trained) are a growth area in the life of the churches.

There is also the need for more trust and support to be given to those specialist youth ministries, such as Youth for Christ and Soul Survivor, who work alongside, but not apart from, the churches.

The Lambeth Conference in 1998, which brought together Anglican bishops from all over the world, called for greatly increased energy and initiative in ministry to young people. My own feeling is that we need to start earlier. Few churches can mount major outreaching work to teenagers today. The cultural gap is huge and the resources are simply not on the ground. I feel we must prayerfully look to para-church agencies to reach some, and trust that God will meet up with others in later life. Most churches, however, can mount effective outreach to children if they have the will to do it, and children will be teenagers in a few years! If we can sow the seed earlier, we may well end up with more to build on and more young people to build it with. We must never forget that the key time when people turn to Christ is before they are in their teens.

* * *

It is fifty years since I was in Charlie Cope's youth group. I have retired and now live near the Norfolk Broads where he used to lead those amazing holidays, with up to fifty teenagers sailing a fleet of hired yachts.

Sometimes I find myself standing on the bank of one of those rivers or Broads, and my mind slips back half a century. In the waterside mist I fancy that I hear again the shouts and the banter. I hear young voices singing Wesley hymns with gusto. I listen in to the crew of one of the yachts as they sit round the cabin discussing a passage of the Bible. And above all I see a small, wiry, cheerful man in a multi-coloured sweater, walking along the bank shouting out some instruction or other. And as I catch an echo of some of the happiest days of my life, I thank God for the chance to have been one of the many who grew up in Charlie Cope's youth group.

4

Called to Order

'Gavin,' said the Reverend Martin Parsons, Vicar of St John's, Blackheath. 'Have you ever thought about ordination?'

It was not the sort of question that the average fifteen-year-old is asked, but that was my age at the time, and that was what my vicar said. I remember feeling somewhat taken aback. My answer was coherent, but only just. I blurted out something about never having stopped thinking about it. It was not strictly true, but my elder brother was about to start ordination training, so it was a subject that had crossed my mind to a moderate degree.

Martin Parsons was a much undervalued parish priest. Nobody thought of him for preferment and his diocese did not honour him with a canonry. He was not someone who sought such things, but I am not the only one who feels that he deserved better.

The reason why his stature and giftedness were ignored was probably to do with the fact that he was an evangelical ministering at the wrong time to be an evangelical. In the 1940s his tradition in the Church of England was treated with a certain amount of lofty disdain. Unlike the present day, evangelicals were conspicuous by their absence from the bench of bishops. Martin, however, a thickset, dark and avuncular man, simply got on with preaching the gospel and caring for the people of his parish. He was a great preacher – in his day one of the best I have ever heard. He had a magnificent deep voice and a good turn of phrase. Above all, he loved the Bible and had a way of making its contents come alive in the pulpit.

He was not a natural young people's man, but we all respected him for his genuineness and his sense of fun. He and his wife Emily modelled a marvellous marriage, and we loved them both for being real people.

So when a man like that turns to one of the teenagers in his church and challenges him about ordination, one could be sure that the words were not spoken casually. I went home thoughtful.

A few weeks later, a large proportion of the congregation was away in Kent on a parish weekend. All ages were present, with the youth fellowship in generous numbers. On the Sunday there was an early morning Communion service in the local parish church and about thirty or so members of our house party attended. I was one of them.

We arrived in good time and waited, some sitting and some kneeling, for the service to begin. I think I was kneeling. It seemed the right sort of thing to do. Then I realized something that almost seemed to hit me in a physical way. With about one minute to go, apart from my group from the house party there was hardly anyone in the church! It was a moment I have never forgotten. I was used to the attendances at a large suburban church. I thought that our church was normal. To see a public service in a parish church with practically no worshippers was like a slap in the face.

I have always said that it was then that I felt I was being

asked about ordination – not by a conscientious vicar, but by God himself. I have always remembered a phrase that came into my mind at the moment when I realized the absence of worshippers: 'What are you going to do about it?'

How much this was my subconscious playing back the result of hidden considerations following Martin Parsons' question, and how much it was a direct act of the Spirit of God, I shall never know and it does not really matter. The Spirit of God can work directly or through people. It is the same Spirit. What I can say is that after that early morning service in a virtually empty church, I have never had any doubts that God wanted me to serve him in some sort of ministry.

For me there could be nothing immediate. I was a school-boy facing what was then called the General Schools Certificate. Three more years in the sixth form followed before a chequered, but ultimately useful, history at London University. It started with me reading geography at Queen Mary College, and it ended with me graduating from Kings College with a degree in philosophy and theology. There followed two years as an education officer in the Royal Air Force, as national service was compulsory in those days.

It was during my national service that I was given leave to attend a selection conference for the ministry. I cannot remember too much about it, except that it was held in Farnham Castle (which was supposed to be haunted) and that one of the selectors was David Say, who was later to be my bishop when I served in the Rochester diocese. I learned soon afterwards that I was recommended for training and that, as they say, was that.

Forty or so years later, the Church has a more elaborate system in place for dealing with those considering the call to ordained ministry. Every diocese has a Diocesan Director of Ordinands (DDO). One of the bishops in each diocese is the sponsoring bishop, and that was one of my responsibilities in Canterbury. Clergy who have potential candidates recommend them to the DDO and there follow interviews, recommended reading and written exercises for the candidates detailing their various spiritual journeys, a local pre-selection conference in many dioceses, and finally the selection conference proper, organized by the Church of England's Ministry Division.

The problem with all this is that it can take a great deal of time between a first inquiry and eventual attendance at a selection conference. Hopes and expectations can be built up, not only in the candidate but also in the congregation from which she or he comes. Failure to be selected can come as a stunning blow.

Rejection is always painful, but it is especially so when that rejection is in effect saying, 'We don't think God wants you for this job.' The most painful area of my work in the Canterbury diocese was having to break the news to people who had not been recommended by the selectors at one of their conferences. Some people took it very badly. The non-recommendation came as a huge blow to their self-confidence. It could also be more than that. We were dealing with people's convictions about God's calling, and non-recommendation could put a question mark over their relationship with God. Some 'failed' candidates found themselves thrown into doubt over the very reality of the God they thought had been calling them to his service. Looking back, I am not sure that I gave them enough support at those painful times.

There was, however, another side to this which we may not find easy to acknowledge, but which remains true nonetheless.

The Church of England, in line with the Catholic tradition, makes much of its priests. They become a group set apart, not only for God but also from the laity. The dynamics of elitism can creep in. Clergy can be seen as the officer class, and this can have an unhealthy appeal to some, muddying their motivation and making their disappointment all the deeper if turned down.

My eight years in the job led me to feel that the Church of England has not quite made up its mind about who actually does the selecting. It sets up what it calls 'selection conferences', and brings together 'selectors' to conduct what I have to admit seems a sound process. The candidates who go to these conferences go feeling certain that it will be make or break time for them. At the same time, however, the Church theoretically recognizes that the diocesan bishop (or the sponsoring bishop if the two are not the same) is the real selector, with the implication that these conferences are simply helping him to do his job. The pool of selectors who serve these conferences have all been nominated by their bishops, although they do not sit in judgement on candidates from their own dioceses. The official letter from the selectors speaks in terms of 'recommending' or 'not recommending' a candidate for training.

For all this talk about the bishop being the real selector, I always felt that the whole process was wrapped up in a culture where it was uncomfortable for the bishop to overturn a non-recommendation. When I was appointed as the archbishop's suffragan bishop and given the sponsoring bishop's job, he encouraged me to see the selectors as advisors only. He encouraged me to exercise my right to select against their advice if necessary. From what I could see, very few bishops did that. Perhaps there is a certain comfort, when dealing with those who are not selected, in presenting oneself simply as a passer-on of bad news. It can be a case of 'don't blame me, I'm only the messenger'.

The fact of the matter is that the Ministry Division, as it is now called, is a very powerful establishment right at the heart of the Church's central structures. Its chief officer is automatically on the Archbishops' Council, which is more than can be said for the chief officers of the Board of Mission or the Board of Education. It regulates which colleges are approved for training and which are not. It draws up the criteria for theological training. It controls the funds that both college (or course) and student need. It has the last word on whether any student in training can go on to work for further qualifications. It regulates the flow of new curates to each diocese (acting, it rightly insists, on behalf of the House of Bishops), and it can force the hand of a diocese on some matters by turning off the supply of cash from its training budget.

There were some times when I felt that a mature candidate on a part-time ordination course, with existing ministerial experience, ought to be made deacon after two years of training. My view was that he or she could complete their final year after being made deacon. Always I would run into a brick wall at this point. The Ministry Division funding for the candidate's training was earmarked for that training which preceded ordination. If the diocese wanted to ordain after two years, then it would have to find the funds for any further training from its own resources. The fact that all the Division's funds came from the dioceses in the first place never seemed to register.

On a number of occasions I did, in fact, set aside the selectors' advice and put a candidate forward for training. It may be that I am paranoic, but I always felt I was under a cloud for doing so. I found that these candidates were treated differently from others. They could not seek a first curacy in another diocese, for example. That could only mean that my selection was not considered to be as 'safe' as the normal choice of the selectors, and yet I was also told that I was recognized as the ultimate selector! As it happened, I was glad that I had to keep my 'overturns' in the diocese. It was reassuring to see that none of them ever let me down.

Does all this mean that the Ministry Division is too big for its boots and that we do not need their selection conferences? I would not want to go that far. I felt a tension with the Division, but I was always glad it was there. I think their conferences are essential. Bishops do indeed need outside perceptions on their candidates. I would have to admit that there were times when the selectors, coming with fresh perspectives, saw things in a candidate that we, who were too close, did not detect. I do think, however, that something is not quite right. A great deal of the problem about the Division rests with the way the Church of England now works, not least the House of Bishops. Bishops have impossible job descriptions. They are being expected to do too many things and to be up to speed on too many agendas. What happens with these sorts of pressures is that the House of Bishops looks to specialized groups of bureaucrats to do their detailed thinking for them. The Ministry Division is one such specialized group, and a very good one.

It will prepare reports, identify criteria for ordinands, inspect the approved training colleges regularly and handle the large budgets that are inevitable with a largely residential training programme. It will do its best to ensure that there is an even quality of approved candidates coming from all the dioceses. It does all these things on behalf of the bishops and puts far more quality time and quality thinking into these matters than lies within the capabilities of most of the bishops. As a result the multiple-agenda-wearied bishops, when they meet, usually nod through most of the recommendations put before them by their bureaucrats. I found myself doing just that myself.

The high quality of the work done by the Division, plus the tiredness of the bishops, usually ended in the Division virtually running things the way they felt best. Always they could say, 'We are only doing what the bishops have asked us to do,' and that would not be untrue. Yet the end result was not completely satisfactory. My continual thought was that the bishops were handing over some areas of responsibility that they should have been keeping to themselves.

The great thing about episcopacy is that the Church, in theory, has the mechanism for very flexible, adaptable and localized decision-making. It should mean that every diocese is run, not by cumbersome representative groupings, but by a person who says his prayers, has his vision, seeks advice, and then has freedom to take initiatives. Of course such a person needs consent for his policies, and that is where the committees and boards have their place. There are, however, still areas where it is advantageous for the bishop to take risks and to break new ground. Nowhere is this more the case than in matters of ministry.

When I was baptized most of the parish churches, large and small, had their stipendiary clergy, resident in their vicarages. That was possible because there were so many trained clergy available, and because there was a culture in the Church that thought it was appropriate to pay their clergy badly. Not only was this culture firmly in place, but there were also enough funds coming from endowments, tithes and the efforts of the

Ecclesiastical Commissioners and Queen Anne's Bounty (later to become the Church Commissioners) to pay for these clergy with little help from church collections. As recently as the 1970s, the budgets of the dioceses had no entries for clergy pay.

Those days are long gone. We now try to pay and to pension our full-time clergy more appropriately, although we still have some distance to travel in this regard. As a result, we have a massive pensions bill to find from central sources, although the parishes are beginning to pay into future pensions. Because of this and other brutal economic facts, the centre can no longer be the paymaster. The parishes and dioceses have to find most of the money for their clergy.

At the same time the numbers of people coming forward for full-time, stipendiary service have dropped seriously from the levels that existed when I began training. The present levels are around 9,000, and expected retirements mean that the numbers must sink lower still. All this poses particular responsibilities for the bishop, because he is the one ultimately responsible for ensuring that there is adequate ministry in every part of 'his' diocese.

This came home starkly to me on one occasion when a candidate from a very remote and rural part of the diocese was 'not recommended' by the selectors. The rural dean, normally a gentle person, pointed out in very strong terms that every candidate for non-stipendiary ministry in his deanery had been turned down in recent years. His population figures were such that there would never be the money to sustain a strong team of stipendiary clergy. Locally generated non-stipendiaries had to be their hope for the future. It was then that I saw something that no detached group of selectors could be expected to see: the need of an area was an important factor in deciding whether someone was called. A doctrine of providence would support this. I set aside the selectors' advice.

I believe that what we need is a more flexible approach towards ministry, towards who gets ordained and how they are trained. No central bureaucracy can operate with that sort of flexibility on behalf of the bishops and their dioceses. It is not fair to expect the Ministry Division to make these sorts of responses, but that is exactly how the Church of England is trying to operate.

Thus we find that schemes for 'ordained local ministry' are being developed, with the intention of allowing congregations to identify natural spiritual leaders in their midst and for such people to be ordained. This purports to be a truly local response to the problem we face, especially in rural dioceses. In fact, a diocese has to put forward a scheme for the approval of the House of Bishops – which, in practice, means the Ministry Division. The concern is that national criteria for selection and training are applied throughout the dioceses. So we are back to 'selectors', 'selection conferences', DDOs doing their pre-selection exercises, and three years of training with strong academic components. Meanwhile, the bishop stands around watching with a feeling of helplessness. The Church's culture of selection and training, developed originally for its stipendiary clergy, still dominates all that happens.

In Canterbury there were several candidates who were already experienced readers and entering their sixties. If they were to become 'ordained local ministers', they would have to undergo three years of further training and at the end of it they would spend a year in deacon's orders, which meant that they would be allowed to do no more in public worship than they were able to do as readers. I found this ridiculous.

Again, if I wanted to ordain them as deacons after two years, with a third year of study after that before priesting, we were back in the familiar funding dry-up. I was told I could make a case for such a move to the Ministry Division, but why on earth should I have to?

When we were considering and debating a move into an ordained local ministry scheme, two particular criticisms were raised on many occasions and with some good cause. The first was whether we were not, in fact, planning to ordain second-class priests who would always be seen as second-class priests. The second was that, if the Church held to the view that a priest was a priest in the whole Church of God, did the limitation to local ministry not make a mockery of this traditional understanding?

There are answers to all these objections, but the fact is that we have a highly unsatisfactory and clumsy situation on our hands. The reason for this clumsiness is that the Church is not being genuinely episcopal in the matter of ministry. No central set of categories for different sorts of priests can deliver the flexibility that is needed on the ground. The best solution is the truly local one, where the bishop decides who gets ordained, how they should be trained and how they should be deployed, always allowing for changes in the scope of deployment.

* * *

In 1995 the archbishop sent me to Chile to represent him in national Anglican celebrations. I went to a small church in a strongly Roman Catholic country. It was financially weak compared to England. It was relatively young – we were celebrating a hundred years of the Anglican mission to the Auracanian Indians of the south. The Church had no cathedrals, no annual synods, no training colleges.

What I found was a vibrant form of Anglicanism that made the Church of England look listless. I discovered that the membership of the Anglican Church in Chile had doubled in the fifteen years leading up to my visit. Above all, I met an approach to selection, training and deployment of clergy that had much to teach me.

Born out of necessity, Chile's Anglican Church identifies and makes decisions about ordination candidates on a case-by-case basis. It only ordains those who have already proved they are ministers and evangelists. Very many of its clergy begin operating as readers. It tailor-makes a training package for every candidate according to ability and experience. If any very intelligent candidates emerge, the Church pays for them to go to another country where there is strong academic training available. Otherwise use is made of its own resources and of what is available in the training institutions of other denominations.

Of course the Church of England is very different from the Anglican Church in Chile. It has a different history, a different relationship to society, and it operates on a much larger scale. It cannot be expected to operate in the same sort of way, but I believe it can learn from the philosophy of selection and training that obtains in Chile.

One thing that I saw very clearly during that visit was that there was none of the status mentality that affects our English ministerial culture. Many of the clergy start unpaid and remain so until the congregations they serve can afford to pay them. At the time I was visiting Chile, the English clergy were involved in discussions about their conditions of service in the ordained ministry as part of a national survey. In contrast, the discussion topics at the meetings of Chilean clergy were about sharing ideas for mission and outreach. Of course they were not perfect and the system had its problems, but I could not avoid the feeling that they made me and my fellow English clergy seem self-centred and status-conscious in comparison.

It was a humbling experience.

5

Serious Training?

Miss Stephanie Sutcliffe, secretary to the principal of Oak Hill College in the 1950s, was a formidable lady. She also had a heart of gold.

Three days after I had begun training for the ministry at Oak Hill, I found myself conscripted into a student gospel group that went out to sing and preach the gospel to young people's clubs in the area. It was led by an amazing character called Jack Filby. Jack had little patience for books and essays, and he was always seeking opportunities to go out and 'do it rather than talk about it'.

So it was that on that Monday evening, armed with a couple of guitars, four of us were standing outside the college gates waiting for a bus to take us into mission. Which is where Miss Sutcliffe came in, or rather, in this event, came out. She crossed the road from the gates to the bus stop and I became aware of an uneasy feeling among the other members of the group. I greeted her innocently and received a guarded smile.

Later, as we tumbled into seats in another part of the bus away from the formidable 'Steffi', Denis Shepheard, another member of the group, muttered something like 'Now we're for it!'

I was completely puzzled. We were a group of grown men. I had only recently been a serving officer in the Royal Air Force. It took me a few minutes to realize that we were, in fact, escaping from the college and doing something naughty. We were not supposed to be out!

I could not believe it. I had come to a college for grown men which that evening I discovered was run like a prep school. I was to learn that it had always been this way. Perhaps this prep school culture dated back to the origins of the college in the 1920s, when it specialized in training men who had little academic background and who, perhaps, needed to be taken back to an educational context that was familiar to them, namely their school classrooms. Whatever the cause, I found it very puzzling and, at times, irritating.

There were others who found it more than simply irritating. One or two were distinctly angry and rebellious. One student, who was later to become an effective and highly responsible parish priest, used to stomp the corridors singing a parody of a children's chorus. It went as follows:

> Oh that will be
> Glory for me . . . glory for me . . . glory for me.
> When by his grace
> I get out of this place . . . that will be glory
> Be glory for me.

As the months rolled by, the rebellion about college restrictions became stronger. If I remember correctly, it came to a head when one or two students complained that there was too much noise in the student wing during study hours. The mood of the student body always became somewhat strained as examinations loomed.

At one such time, a particularly tense student decided to pray about things out loud in the weekly college prayer meeting. 'Help us to remember, O Lord,' he said, with one particular student in mind, 'that we must not run up and down the corridors and we must not use our typewriters in our studies.'

Denis Shepheard, a cheery former sailor, was kneeling next to the only person known to run noisily up and down corridors. In his pious position he leaned sideways and whispered, 'Got yer tin 'at on, mate?'

The principal, a delightful man called Leslie Wilkinson, affectionately known as 'Wilkie', felt that things had to be brought to a head and that the riot act had to be read. He was a kindly and very humorous man himself, but he felt that he had a job to do and that the college culture had to be maintained. At the end of lunch one day, he rose and addressed the student body. We were reminded that discipline was part of the life of a Christian minister, and that college had its rules and they were there to be obeyed. He reminded us that the period between 7.00 and 9.15 in the evening was for study, and that all of us were expected to be in our rooms and at our books. His peroration included something that exposed the daftness of the whole business. 'We need absolute quiet during that time,' he said. 'There should be no need for even the sound of lavatories being flushed!'

Immediately little groups of people plotted an appropriate response. I suggested to a number of people that on the dot of 9.15 that evening, every single loo should be flushed throughout the college to the accompaniment of loud and relieved cheering. And it was so. Another group arranged things so that, as we trooped from our studies to the dining room for late-night drinks, we found ourselves walking past a table full of chamber pots with a notice saying 'FOR HIRE'.

Tom Walker, fresh from Oxford and later to become an archdeacon, went to see the principal. Tom's gentle and artistic exterior masked a steely resolve and the courage of a lion. Not for him silly protests with jerries. He told Wilkie that this was a college of grown men, many of whom had held responsible positions before coming to college. He said that the regime at Oak Hill was the reason why so few Oxbridge graduates would look at the place. He suggested that the regime needed to be eased considerably, because it was souring an otherwise happy and positive community.

Shortly afterwards, we were all summoned to the chapel. Wilkie stood up with astonishing grace and announced that we needed to help each other find a new culture for the community life of the college. Whatever we may have learned from our books and lectures, I think we learned more about the graciousness of a Christian minister at that moment than at any other time.

Every day we would be up early for chapel before breakfast. A bell would summon us, and each week a student would be detailed to act as bell steward. The bell rope actually passed through the principal's flat, which was above the main hall and assembly area. One day the bell steward slept in and, on waking, flung on his clothes and dashed to the hall, only to find that the bell was already tolling. As he got to the hall, all he could see was the rope going up and down but with no one holding it. He was found leaning against a wall, ashen faced, watching the apparition – little realizing that the principal had decided to take matters into his own hand in the flat above.

Chapel remained compulsory, and I think we all knew that

this was right. For all the easing of regulations, Oak Hill remained, in my time, a community of people preparing for future ministry together. We worshipped together and we ate together, and when someone hit hard times, most of us felt involved.

Things have changed tremendously in the years since I left Oak Hill. The Church takes training and qualifications far more seriously. The academic quality of theological college staffs is significantly higher, as are the academic expectations placed on the students. At the same time, the style of learning and evaluation has changed.

For a few years in the mid-1990s I was invited to spend several days every year teaching a module on evangelism at one of our colleges. I well remember my first morning. I was in the college guest room, and I discovered that there was no chapel before breakfast. When I came down to the dining room for breakfast, I found it virtually empty. A few students, mostly from overseas, were sitting round one of the tables and getting up from time to time to help themselves to coffee or to put bread slices in the toaster. The combination of a modular approach to training, where people picked this or that component and thereby this or that hour of attendance, and the fact that many were older students living off campus with their families, had made a profound difference. In my visits to the college over the next few years I could see little evidence of a community of friends preparing together for future ministry. There was a system of fellowship groups, which I am sure were important, but the sense of the whole body being a fellowship seemed less obvious.

If I was right in this judgement, another factor was largely responsible. Financial reasons encourage the colleges to grow bigger and have more students paying their fees each year. The college where I lectured had students from other countries and other denominations. I could immediately see positive outworkings from such a mix. Nevertheless, I was left feeling that the precise focus we had in Oak Hill, where we all knew we were preparing for the same task in the same organization, had been lost.

Learning at Oak Hill in the 1950s was more formal than it is today. It was basically about lectures, tutorials, essay-writing and examinations. The truth was, however, that much of the learning at Oak Hill took place informally, outside the classroom and away from books and essays. It took place in unstructured conversations between groups of us, and especially after lunch when everyone broke up into 'coffee schools'.

The Oak Hill coffee schools were a feature of college life in my day, and they tended to develop distinctive characteristics and even names. The one I belonged to became known as the 'Hot Pot Coffee School', on account of the large percolator that one of our number owned. We boasted that we always had 'real' coffee and that we were the only coffee school that talked serious theology. I am sure the latter boast was an exaggeration, but we were privileged to have Anthony Thiselton, a future professor of theology at Nottingham University, as a member.

Over our coffee (real indeed, but rather insipid) we would often wrestle with genuine theological conundrums, and we would certainly put the Church and the world to rights at regular intervals. It was a stimulating group to belong to and it made for a continuous learning experience that was an invaluable addition to the college syllabus. We were also pretty good at producing hilarious items for the college's annual Christmas concert – usually requiring Thiselton to turn up in an amazing range of costumes. We never did find out how he got hold of them.

Oak Hill was, and remains, one of a number of theological colleges in England which are recognized by the Church as appropriate places to train for ordination. The colleges, however, have never been an integral part of the Church of England itself. They are independent institutions, founded and run by trusts and committees determined to maintain particular traditions in the Church. The Church of England has, broadly speaking, three main traditions within itself. There is the Evangelical tradition, which has two main inspirations: the sixteenth-century Reformation and the eighteenth-century Evangelical Awakening. There is the Catholic tradition, which dates back to the insights and emphases of the nineteenth-century Oxford Movement. Between these two lies a more liberal and less well defined strand that again dates back to inspirations in the latter half of the nineteenth century and the early decades of the twentieth. The different colleges prepare candidates for ordination in ways that reflect the differing emphases of these traditions. Today a rigorous system of inspections organized by the Ministry Division demands and ensures high and even standards across all the colleges.

Oak Hill was firmly in the Evangelical tradition. Unkind observers would describe it as the lowest of the low church. Students in my time found it difficult to decide whether the Catholics or the Liberals were the greater enemy, but enemies they were. Lines were fiercely drawn, and the Catholics and Liberals were seen to be firmly in the ascendancy in the nationwide Church at that time. Things were very tribal.

It is not surprising that there have always been voices in the Church that lament this approach to training for the ministry.

In a Church where these traditions need to work in harmony, it is not unreasonable to wonder whether we would be better served if the colleges were not so clearly aligned, and if they were to contain staff members who represented the full spectrum of Church tradition. The latest thinking about the future of theological education has even considered replacing the existing colleges with one or two central, non-aligned colleges.

In the last thirty years a greater flexibility of approach to ministry and training has developed. We now have a large number of people in secular employment offering for part-time ministry as priests. This has led to the development of part-time training courses in different parts of the country, and this time these institutions are run directly by the various dioceses. Such courses are intended to be broader based than the colleges, with teaching and preparation coming from people who represent all the schools of thought within the Church.

While I believe that we will have to move away from such heavy reliance on three-year residential courses, I am not convinced that the non-residential courses self-evidently do a better job out of their broader bases. In fact, I am not convinced that their bases are all that broad. My own tradition, Evangelicalism, is widely recognized as the fastest-growing tradition in the Church, with over half our ordination candidates coming from its parishes. Yet evangelical input on the staffs of the courses does not reflect this strength on the ground. There is no skulduggery in this. The courses have tiny staffs and have to rely on a large number of parish clergy, and others, with academic strings to their bows. The truth is that evangelicals tend to be activists rather than reflectives, and even when they have theological expertise they usually prefer to bury themselves in pastoral and evangelistic ministry.

I remain convinced that the Church is better off for its various traditions, as long as those within them see their task to be that of witnessing to precious insights rather than fighting against the insights of others. At its best, the Church of England is a place of creative internal dialogue, and this can be enlivening and stimulating. In the time since my own ordination in 1960, the various traditions have increasingly listened more carefully to each other and there has been a considerable amount of cross-fertilization and mutual respect.

My main reason for supporting the present system of colleges with churchmanship emphases is that they can prepare people for ministry from a coherent platform of thought and practice. They send their candidates into the ministry with operational understandings that make sense to them. This has the effect of keeping the theological and ministerial dialogue alive in the Church. It does not, contrary to some allegations, mean that the products of college training are inflexible robots. They do change and they do become more flexible, but they do this from the inner security of their roots. The last thing we need is some sort of centrally imposed ecclesiastical social engineering in our training.

The real problem with the college system is not the diversity of theologies that it reflects. The real problem is the cost of residential training. It costs the Church £9 million a year to prepare its ministers. While that sum covers the cost of the courses as well as the colleges, and while the numbers training on the courses are almost as many as those in the colleges, inevitably residential training is more expensive, costing about twice as much per candidate. This ministry training figure is the largest single item in the Church's budget, and it makes sense to ask whether the Church is getting value for money.

In the final decade of the twentieth century, attendance in the Church of England dropped by over 20 per cent. It may well be that the reasons for this are complex, and it is fair to point out that most other denominations showed similar trends. Nevertheless, any business faced with a 20 per cent drop in customers would ask whether it was going about things in the best way. Are we really so sure that we are sending men and women into the ministry prepared in the best way to serve the Church in a missionary age?

Writing of the situation in the 1970s, Professor Adrian Hastings said, 'The majority of the clergy in all the churches seemed to have next to no idea how to cope with the frankly missionary situation which now faced them.'[1] Hastings could well be reflecting on the situation that still obtains. I have found it surprising that so few seriously ask whether we know how to train modern priests for the missionary task ahead of them.

In 1974 I began my work as an advisor in evangelism, working with the Church Pastoral Aid Society. I would travel round the country, listening to those who seemed to have found out how to be more effective in drawing new people into their congregations and helping them to understand the gospel. I would try to formulate what I had been hearing and seeing, and I would try to pass it on in seminars and lectures, in articles and in a book. I was simply trying to teach the logistics that needed to be put in place if congregations were to grow and if people were to come to faith. What I had to say was pretty basic and commonplace, yet everywhere I went I met people who found what I was doing to be refreshing and novel. Nobody I met in the Church of England's ministry had been trained in these logistical matters when they were in

[1] A. Hastings, *A History of English Christianity 1920–85*, (Collins), p. 615.

college or on one of the courses. They may have had some teaching of theory, *but they had received very little actual teaching of pastoral and evangelistic practice.*

To be fair, the colleges are under immense pressures. With the unchallenged assumption everywhere that academic standards and qualifications are vital, their priorities in pre-ordination training have been to bring their students to levels of competence that could be recognized by external examiners. The name of the game has become the granting of respectable and recognized academic qualifications. For small staffs facing mixed-ability classes this is a very demanding task, and it is to the immense credit of those who run the colleges and courses that they achieve such high standards and merit such university accreditation. Surely, however, it cannot be foolish to ask whether this is the best way to train people to lead churches, to preach the gospel, to train others to engage in continuous mission and to know how to pastor as well as to help others to be pastoral?

When we train teachers, much time is spent ensuring that they know how to operate in a classroom. Of course academic ability has to be there, and the education of our educators is an obvious first step. No person, however, can operate in a classroom simply because he or she knows the subject that is supposed to be taught. Teachers have to know the 'how to' of teaching. Similarly, no soldiers are sent into battle with a training that stops at the theory of ballistics. They have to know how to fire a gun and they have to have pre-battle experience of doing so. It was when I trained as an officer in the Royal Air Force that I first heard the word 'logistics', and the logistics of engaging in pastoral mission is where the Church is weakest. We are good at talking, but we are not good at translating the talk into effective action.

I believe the Church of England knows how to *educate*, but I am less sure that we have fully mastered how to *train*. Although every college and course has someone in charge of 'pastoral studies', I am not aware of any serious attempt to make the teaching of the principles and practice of pastoral mission a discipline with recognized standards.

Preaching and other forms of communication require particular attention. Whether we like it or not, most people only engage with the content of our faith in Sunday sermons. It would be good if they would all enrol in midweek classes, or come earlier for 'all-age Sunday school' as they often do in America, but private reading and sermons are the main inputs for British Christians – with private reading coming a poor second.

There can surely be no gainsaying the importance of turning out clergy who can hold attention, communicate and inspire. The problem is that preaching is not a subject that sits comfortably with academic accreditation. It is not, therefore, a high priority on the timetable. A further problem is that the Church of England has never taken preaching seriously, and there is a shortage of people with the ability and understanding to teach the 'how to' of preaching.

Those responsible for ordination training have a ready answer when challenged about the need to train people in pastoral and evangelistic practice. They tell us that such matters are best learned in the context of the training parish. Apparently, a good training vicar is the answer to the problem. This, however, begs the all-important question: where do these marvellous training vicars learn good practice? The answer, presumably, is that they learned these all-important matters in turn from the vicars who trained them.

All of this highlights the fact that we bring considerable professionalism into the theological preparation of our clergy, but something more akin to amateurism when it comes to the practice of ministry. I think we can do better than that. If the bishops were to ask for pastoral and evangelistic practice to be made a discipline in this way, I believe there is the skill in the Ministry Division to make it happen.

Some years ago, I was asked to share my thoughts on training, as an outsider, with the staff of St John's College, Nottingham, one of our larger training colleges. I remember suggesting that the colleges should offer a one-year residential foundation course which was compulsory for all candidates. With that year behind them, they should be ordained deacon, perhaps for two years, and sent to their first parish. In their first two years they should return to a college (not necessarily the same one) for two five-week courses a year. Ordination to the priesthood would be dependent on such further training. For a further three years, all clergy would be required to return to a college for at least one further five-week unit each year.

The advantages I saw from this approach were that it would move people more quickly into ministry. It would also build in a regime of in-service training which would be compulsory at first, but would hopefully encourage voluntary returns to colleges for five-week units on various subjects thereafter. Diocesan CME (Continuous Ministerial Education) Officers could monitor and advise as to the value of this or that unit and this or that college. I also felt that the shortness of the courses would remove the need for students to seek married accommodation in and around the colleges and thus cause less disruption to families. Even in the initial residential year (three ten-week terms) there could be frequent free weekends.

My hope also was that this would strengthen the role of the colleges, as they would become places of pre- and post-ordination training and centres of excellence. At present the dioceses have their individual arrangements, the quality of which varies from place to place. With my proposals, I felt, we might be able to save effort and, possibly, money at diocesan level.

I think that my hearers at St John's were pretty bemused by my efforts as I spelled out my vision. However, over twenty years later, I still feel this would be a better way to ensure that we have a well-trained ministry – although I now think that the residential year should be preceded by a period of training by extension, with each student studying at home for a year or so before going to college.

At the moment we front-load our training to such a degree that all subsequent training suffers, and students are prepared too far away from the theatre of action. A concentrated three-year residential training programme can encourage people to feel that they have been there, done it, and require nothing more. I have found that those who have completed their three years of institutionalized training are often resentful of the local post-ordination training laid on in the dioceses. My proposal is for a lighter pre-ordination component, followed by more serious post-ordination elements over the next few years. This might create a culture of continuous reflection and study relating to the task, and could remove the need for sabbaticals. There would also be a very desirable plus-factor: we would be training our clergy 'on the job' to a much greater degree.

* * *

Over the years I have rarely returned to Oak Hill. My last visit was to preach. I was Bishop of Maidstone by then. I cannot remember what my sermon was about, and I do not think it was one of my best. What I can remember is stepping into the pulpit and catching sight of the text that looks up at every preacher who preaches to the college community. The text is written very clearly on a small inlaid plaque. It says: '*Sirs, we would see Jesus.*'

That has to be the ultimate goal of any training course, yet it is something that no university accreditation could ever guarantee. We need men and women in the ministry who not only have developed the skills to communicate Christ, but whose lives are such that Christ can be seen in them.

6

Parish Realities

When my mind cleared, I realized it was nearly five to eight in the morning. It was Sunday. I was the curate of St Paul's, East Ham, and it was my turn to take the eight o'clock Communion service. I had slept in.

I went through the mockery of a shave and wash, flung on my clothes and ran to the church, entering, as I always did, by way of the adjoining hall. It was after eight and I could hear that the vicar, Dick Browning (later to become an honorary canon of Worcester), had already started. I was too late. I had let him down.

As a penance I put out the chairs for the Pathfinder classes to be held later that morning. The service ended and the door from the church opened into the vestry where I was standing. Dick looked at me with the suspicion of a smile and said, 'There, but for the grace of God, go all of us!' I was forgiven.

On reflection, I have sometimes wondered whether Dick was too undemanding a 'training vicar' as far as I was concerned. We started with the disadvantage of being close friends. He probably should have pulled me up more often than he did. In fact, I can think of only one occasion in our three years together when he actually spoke sharply to me.

We had first met at a boys' camp run by the Church Pastoral Aid Society in the early 1950s. I was a sixth-former, and he was training for the ministry at the London College of Divinity. I was a very junior tent officer, and he was the sports officer. I found him a fun person and great to be with, but the demands of sixty boys ensured that we did not get too much time to chat together.

Curiously enough, we next met a few years later at another sort of camp. To be precise, it was a Pathfinders house party in Felixstowe in 1955. Dick was by then serving his first curacy in east London, and I was reading philosophy and theology at Kings College, London. At the house party I was a dorm officer, and Dick held the exalted role of adjutant, the second-in-command. How we all loved military terms in those days!

This time we did get more opportunity to talk together, and a firm friendship began. A few months later he was asked to lead a similar house party the following year, and he contacted me to ask if I would be his adjutant. We had to put a new team together and he was desperately short of a kitchen team. I recommended a nurse friend of mine who was the sort of person who would embrace any challenge. Her name was Paddy (Patricia) Young. She later became Paddy Browning, and I was best man at the wedding ceremony.

By the time June 1960 came along, I was not only Dick's friend and colleague from several boys' camps, and the man who had introduced him to his wife – I was his curate.

Early morning Communion services were apt to be times of

trial for me. I remember one Sunday morning when it was my duty to read the epistle for the day. I am afraid I had not checked it through beforehand, and this led to my undoing. As I began reading, my eye – as these things can happen – fell on the fact that in a few lines' time I was going to come face to face with the word 'concupiscence'. I had a premonition that it might be a painful experience. The nearer I came to that word, the more I had this ominous feeling. When I reached the line, I decided that attack was the best way to deal with things.

I charged into it: 'Not in the lusts of cup . . .' No, that was the second syllable. I started again. 'Not in the lusts of cucon . . .' Oh dear, wrong again. I became aware of greater than usual attention from the congregation. One more time. 'Co . . . co . . .' I gave up, said a quick 'sence', and moved on.

I am sorry to say that the congregation of St Paul's, East Ham, were now highly amused at the thought of 'the lusts of concupiscence', which was exactly what St Paul was trying to discourage.

The first time I had to chant the versicles and responses was also a daunting experience. I am not musically literate, although I think I can hold a tune. I had rehearsed the versicles before the service, and I was sure that I would be all right. As the service proceeded, however, I became less sure. Then the moment arrived. The organist gave me the note. 'O Lord, open thou our lips,' I sang, and pretty well too.

The congregation, little dreaming of my self-doubt, belted back, 'And our mouth shall show forth thy praise!'

This was good! We were rolling. I let them have, 'O God, make speed to save us,' and I was still in tune. Again the response came strongly back. We were now on our feet as I sang the next line, 'Glory be to the Father, and to the Son, and to the Holy Ghost.' Back came the response. Finally I sang, still in tune, 'Praise ye the Lord!' Back came the reply, 'The Lord's name be praised!' I had done it! Huge relief . . .

I was still standing, and so was the choir, and the congregation, and Dick immediately opposite me in his stall. There was silence as people waited for the next ministerial prompt. Suddenly I realized that they were waiting for me! I had to announce the psalm, and I could not remember what it was. I looked down at my service sheet to see the number, but all I saw was a whole spinning flux of numbers – hymn numbers, psalm numbers, Bible reference numbers. I could not focus quickly enough, so I played for time. 'We shall sing . . .' I announced, but still I could not isolate the psalm number.

I decided to be honest. 'Frankly,' I said, 'I don't know what we shall sing!'

Grinning broadly, the Vicar of St Paul's came to the rescue as vicars do. Someone said to me afterwards that it was the best thing I had done since arriving in the parish. Everyone now knew I was human, and in their warm, east London way, they became my friends.

St Paul's was a great place to serve a first curacy. It had a fun-loving but totally committed vicar, and it was full of unpretentious, down-to-earth people. They were typical Eastenders with plenty of humour. In a remarkable way, it was a congregation that had grown through the preaching of Billy Graham in his great crusades of 1954 and 1955. The vicar at the time had backed the crusades more than any of the other parish churches in the borough. Parties had been taken to the meetings and people had responded, while others living in the area, who had gone to the meetings by other means and had also responded, were referred to St Paul's by the organizers. I remember that the house next to the vicarage contained a convert from the missions, as did the house next door to that, and another some three or four doors further along.

The streets were packed with terraced houses. The residents were often dockers or Ford workers from nearby Dagenham. They were not poor, but most could remember hard times in the past. They counted their blessings and were positive people. Most of them were 'workforce' rather than 'management', and this tended to show in the meetings of the church council. I shall never forget my first Parochial Church Council (PCC) meeting in a room in the vicarage – the only double-fronted house in the parish. Dick was in the chair and he led us all in brief opening devotions. Everyone seemed in good spirits.

Then we turned to the agenda, and everything changed. Very quickly I could see what was happening. Dick had become 'management' and everyone else was 'workforce'. Almost every item became a battle royal, and there were times when Dick was accused of lack of consultation and various other examples of bad management. I watched the proceedings with growing alarm. Then it came to the closing prayer and the inevitable tea and biscuits. Everybody was fine. 'Good meeting, wasn't it, Gavin?' someone said with a broad smile. As I looked around, it became clear that everyone had, indeed, thoroughly enjoyed the evening.

As often happened with curates, I was put in charge of the young people's work. There was much to do. Every Sunday morning, upwards of a hundred youngsters under fourteen were in church. Curiously, the morning service was not attended by the adults, so everything was tailored to the requirements of these youngsters. Dick was very gifted with this age group and he was rightly concerned that we should hold them into and through their teenage years.

The older young people met on Friday evenings, and they were a lively group. The previous curate warned me to look out for a particular youngster called David. In fact, David turned out to be outstanding, ending up as a bank manager with Barclays and a pillar of his local church. Most of the young people turned up for the Sunday evening service and generally brought a bit of life to the place. We would hold an after-church meeting tackling serious themes in various ways. It was not long before Mary and I declared open house for the young people on Tuesday evenings, and this gave us a chance simply to get to know them and talk over whatever they wanted to discuss. There was no attempt at a programme.

There were times when the youth fellowship fell foul of powerful people in the congregation. One charge, not without reason, was that the youngsters damaged the church hall with their boisterous games on Friday evenings. Chairs got broken on occasion and scratches would appear on the paintwork. I can remember being called to defend what I was doing at a PCC meeting. I felt pretty angry at what seemed to be the short-sightedness of those complaining. Many churches, I thought, would be only too grateful to have such a promising group of youngsters. Alas, I found that there were people who were only too quick to say that all young people were going to the dogs, and who lumped our youngsters into this judgement.

I remember speaking quite emotionally to the PCC about the situation. I pointed out that if Christ was prepared to give his life for all of us, surely we, for our part, could accept the odd broken chair. Eastenders understand emotion. I ended up with a vote of confidence. Later I discovered that Paddy had been eavesdropping on that item and praying for me from the other side of the room's serving hatch. One of the chief complainers came up to me afterwards and offered his car and his services if we wanted to do car maintenance as a club activity. It was a generous response, and a sign of healing.

Some time later, tensions re-emerged around the time of the annual general meeting of the PCC. I decided to enrol every eligible youth club member on the electoral roll. They packed the meeting and voted in members whom they believed would be more supportive of their cause. People took it in good part, but the annual meeting for the next year produced a record attendance!

There was another group of young people in the area who never joined in with our church activities. Their ringleader lived a few doors away from us. Most of the gang had been in trouble with the police at some time. One Sunday the mother of the ringleader – we shall call him Mick – knocked on our door at lunchtime. She and Mick lived alone, and she was often out until late in the evening. People told me that when Mick had been younger it was not unknown to see him huddled in the doorway of his house, waiting for his mother to come home and let him in. Not surprisingly, the relationship was very bad. That Sunday, Mick's mother was clearly in a fearful condition. 'Mick's got a gun and bullets, and he's threatening to kill me!' she said. 'He's digging a big hole in the garden and he says it's for me. Can you come and take his gun away?'

They do not train you in theological college for moments like that! I left my lunch and walked down to her house, hoping that somehow I would find a way of dealing with the situation. I am sure I prayed! When I got to the house, I found that Mick was brandishing a powerful air rifle. I also found that he had a few rounds of .22 bullets. I became braver on the spot. There was no way those bullets would fit that rifle. I spoke to Mick – it was the first time we had spoken to each other – and I suggested that, as his mother was in a state and the police could get called in, it might be useful if I looked after his gun for a few days. He agreed.

Mick and his friends began to come to the Tuesday night open house sessions. They mixed with our regulars and got on fairly well. One night, one of them picked up a loose-leaf notebook which was on my desk. He noticed that it contained several pages with lists of names on them. On one page he found his own name. 'Here,' he said. 'What's all this?'

I explained that he was looking at my prayer diary and that I had been praying for him and his friends. The mood changed remarkably. A discussion followed which led to Mick's gang coming round to our house later that week for a long chat on 'this Jesus business'. When they arrived, we were in some disarray. Mary had been whisked into the maternity hospital for baby number two. Her mother had moved in to hold the fort and was feeling distinctly uneasy about my visitors. We bought in ten shillings' worth of chips (which was a great deal in those days) and brewed frequent cups of instant coffee, and the discussion continued until the early hours. I found I had to go back to basics and simply talk them through the story of Jesus. When I got to the point in the story where Jesus cried out from the cross, 'Father, forgive them,' one of the boys laughed. He could not believe that anyone in that situation would do anything other than curse his tormentors.

Today, nearly forty years later, I still remember that amazing encounter. I cannot remember how many times I have preached the gospel in evangelistic missions and meetings, but I sometimes wonder whether that evening over coffee and chips was the only time in my ministry when I truly 'did the work of an evangelist'.

The day came when Mick was arrested for loitering in a shop front armed with a housebreaking implement. It had been in the early hours of the morning. He had walked his girlfriend home – we will call her Sally – after a long party at his home, made possible because his mother was away. I was in court when the case came up, hoping to say something helpful by way of a character reference. I became deeply disturbed at what was happening.

Mick was challenged that it was far too late at night for his story about walking Sally home after a party to be believable. I knew he was telling the truth. After all, the party had been taking place only a few doors away from my house. I could hear it.

Worse was to follow. The 'housebreaking implement' was no more than a glove. I could see, however, that it was Sally's glove. I wanted to shout to Mick in the court and suggest that he demonstrate that it did not fit him. Mick was not capable of thinking that clearly. He was found guilty, and as he had past form he was sent to a detention centre. I got my chance to say something positive about him, but it was to closed minds, after the guilty verdict.

I left court angry with what had happened. It was not to be the last time that I would appear in court and watch a youngster get a raw deal. The tragedy is that, when a young person has a record of offences to his or her name, it is very difficult to persuade police and magistrates that they might be trying to reform. I can see that an overworked police force can make mistakes and that it is not easy (or always desirable) for them to believe the best in dubious situations.

When Mick was sent down, Sally was distraught. The only people she felt she could trust were the young people from the church she had met on Tuesday evenings. On the Sunday after the trial, she came with them to church. As she came through the door she was handed a hymn book by our very respectable churchwarden, Jack Smith. I watched with a lump in my throat as, to her surprise, he said quietly, 'Hello, Sally . . .' He had taken the trouble to find out. I think those two words spoke more about the love of God than any sermon.

Some time after Mick had finished his sentence, he married Sally in St Paul's. She was pregnant. I took the service. At the reception all the men watched the Grand National on the television. Mick has never been in trouble with the police since that day. He held down a job until bad health intervened, and raised a family.

I lost contact with them until 1999, when a Christmas card came through the door from Sally. She had seen me on television and found out my address. Her note was cheerful and movingly affectionate towards Mary and me. They may not have clocked into church very much, if at all, since those days in the 1960s, but God had been at work. All he needed was someone like that churchwarden and those youngsters at St Paul's.

No statistical analysis will ever measure the sort of story I have just told. Mick and Sally do not show in church attendance statistics, but their lives are known to God. There are some 13,000 Church of England parishes throughout the country, to say nothing of the thousands of other Christian congregations. In every church, and as a result of the work and presence of thousands of Christian ministers and congregations, stories like that of Mick and Sally can be told again and again. When press reports appear to glory in the follies and failures of the Churches, they seem to be totally unaware of the hidden reconciling ministry that is always taking place.

The people of St Paul's expected a good sermon, and they were not too bothered about length. That said, there were limits. I remember leading an evening service with a West African preacher. After forty minutes he said, 'Secondly . . .' I think he pushed his luck a little.

Dick Browning was a good and conscientious preacher. He was even better when he was less tied to his notes. Like many of us, however, and certainly myself, he felt most comfortable when he was looking down at a fairly full script. One Sunday, he was relying on a clear afternoon to finish his evening sermon. Alas, this was not to be the case. Several calls on his time came out of the blue, and he entered the pulpit that evening with two scripted points and a third section that was, if anywhere, in his head. He came through with flying colours and I overheard one of the faithful saying admiringly, 'Wasn't Dick inspired tonight? He didn't look at his notes once in that last section.' Well observed! What she did not realize was that Dick had absolutely nothing to look down at.

St Paul's was the only church I knew where you could be criticized for preaching too short. You could also be criticized at the church door if you were incomprehensible, or if some astute Eastender simply thought you were talking rubbish. I remember one Ford worker taking me aside after a sermon on 'witness'. 'Gavin,' he said, 'you go on about how we must talk about Jesus to our mates at work. Have you ever worked on an assembly line? You talk, and you hold things up and everyone loses wages!'

St Paul's had a branch of the Mothers' Union, and its banner could be seen prominently in the chancel at all times, except when it was being carried triumphantly in procession at Mothers' Union festival services around the deanery. When I arrived, the Mothers' Union were agonizing over the rather dowdy condition of their banner. It seemed fine to my untutored eyes, but apparently it did not acquit itself well when compared to other banners at these deanery occasions. 'It's a bad witness,' members were told at one of their meetings, and this judgement met with widespread agreement.

The banner was duly refurbished for the princely sum of £40, which was a great deal of money in those days. The big day came when a Mothers' Union patronal festival service was to take place at a nearby parish, and the new banner was to go on show for the first time. Dick and I made sure we were there to see the great sight.

There was a well-established ritual with these banners. Three representatives from each Mothers' Union branch in the deanery, dressed in nurse-like blue headdresses, would accompany each banner, one holding the banner and one on either side. At the beginning of the service the banner parties would process to the front of the church. The officiating clergy would take the banners and arrange them against the east wall of the sanctuary. At the end of the service the parish representatives would again walk forward to receive their banners back, before solemnly processing out. The trick for the officiating clergy was to ensure that each banner party received the same banner at the end of the service. This was a trick that was not always mastered.

I must record that, on the great day when our new banner had its first outing, our St Paul's banner party walked back down the aisle bearing not only the wrong banner but the tattiest banner available, and looking as if there was a nasty smell somewhere close to their noses! I also have to record that, faced with this first-order tragedy, the Vicar of St

Paul's was standing at the back scarcely able to control his mirth.

* * *

First curacies are supposed to be learning times. What did I learn at St Paul's? Some might feel that a great deal of this is pretty trivial. Talk of banners and arguments on church councils all seems very far removed from the greatest cause in history. Sleeping in when I should have been taking services and making a hash of Evensong hardly square with the call to evangelize the world. So much that happens in the average parish church seems rather petty. The New Testament, we think, speaks of sterner stuff.

All this may be true, but the fact is that pettiness, arguments and getting banners mixed up are all things that one would expect from real people trying to get on together. We tend to look at the New Testament through rose-coloured spectacles. There was plenty of pettiness among the Lord's disciples. The dramatically expanding church of the Acts of the Apostles was not without its arguments and people having to fight their corner in church council meetings. Real people may well do great and heroic things, but they also tend to get banners out of proportion and grumble about chipped paint in the church hall.

Real people also marry, have babies, endure illnesses and disappointments, and eventually die. Those years in East Ham moved me into a world that many avoid – the world of embracing suffering. No pastor can avoid living in that world. Some years ago a friend of mine was a vicar in St Helen's, famous for its rugby league team – a tough game for tough men. One day he was walking past the crowd waiting for the gates to open at the St Helen's ground. 'Come on in, Vicar!' shouted someone. 'Come and see some real life!' My friend stopped. 'I'd love to,' he said. 'Unfortunately, I've got to go and see a dying man, and then I've got to see a widow and tell her that her son has just been arrested and is likely to end up in jail. What's that you said about real life?'

My time in East Ham was indeed a learning period. I suppose I went there expecting to be the teacher and the inspiration for others, but the truth was exactly the reverse. The people of St Paul's taught me about discipleship and love for God. They were in their pews Sunday after Sunday. They did not have to be, and many of their neighbours thought they were dotty to do it. They were people who knew what it was to need encouragement, and they also knew how to give it. They were people who had mostly lived through hard times. Dockers used to tell me of the bad old days when they had been unable to get work at the dock gates. Because of such a past, they knew how to count their blessings and enjoy them.

They brought to their Christianity a refreshing absence of veneer. What you saw was what there was. If they felt angry, they told you. If they thought you were being conceited, they told you. If they felt they had been out of order, they owned up. If they felt you had done a good job, they told you so. If they believed that Jesus was special, they did not keep it to themselves.

Many of them were first-generation regular worshippers. They were blissfully ignorant of middle-class, churchy respectability. They laughed in church if you gave them a chance. They enjoyed a good sing. They booby-trapped the pulpit at Christmas. They argued with the vicar after the service, but it was always an argument between friends.

From Dick Browning I learned many things also. He brought fun into ministry and released the sense of fun that seems natural to Eastenders. He allowed people to be themselves. He was imaginative and loved drama. The Christmas services had a touch of magic. I will always remember that our carol service was decorated by candles set in logs which were coated with sugar to look wintry. We had a conscientious fire officer in the congregation, and the sight of naked flames approaching sugar-coated logs totally spoiled his Christmas worship every year. Good Friday was a great time for drama, and one year half the congregation was roped into a passion play that packed the church.

Youth and children's work was the engine room of the church. Dick loved working with children. It was not a ministry to be left to elderly ladies. The clergy were expected to take a lead, and plenty of young adult energy was invested. Today, as we have noted, some 40 per cent of our parish churches have no children's ministry and even more are without any work among teenagers. Unless that changes, the Church of England faces a precarious future.

When I moved on from St Paul's, it was to a new housing area in Essex, a newly built church and a small, heroic, but overstretched congregation. I tried to impress them that they had a leader in their midst and, for a number of reasons, kept my own sense of fun under wraps. It was not long before the local doctor was prescribing Valium to get me through the day. As I reflected on the situation, I felt that God was saying something. It was something that took me back to what I had learned at St Paul's. 'The people here are finding church very hard work,' I felt God saying to me. 'They need a good laugh. That's why I brought you here. Be yourself!'

In my eight years as a bishop I sometimes wished that I

could send one of 'my' priests back in a time warp to the St Paul's of old. Whether it be to learn the place of imagination, or the value of preaching, or the importance of fun, or the need to be yourself, or simply to find that if you love people they will love you back – St Paul's had so much to teach. The Church of England is right to insist that all its clergy are apprenticed to a vicar and a parish as the conclusion of their training. The only problem with this strategy is that you need the right vicar and the right parish. I was lucky on both counts.

7

The Evangelicals

Westminster Chapel was a strange meeting place for a large number of Anglicans, but on that cold January Saturday morning in 1995 it was packed to the doors with them.

I remember the day well. It started when Mary and I woke up in our far from sumptuous room in the Strand Palace Hotel. We had booked in on a theatregoer's special, and this was strangely appropriate. What took place in the Westminster Chapel had a great deal of theatre about it.

I recall sitting up in bed reading and revising my script for the umpteenth time. I had been working on it for months, which was something very unusual for me. Then again, I was quite sure (and remain so) that I was about to deliver the most important address I would ever give in my life. Quite simply, the conference had been called to try to save the Evangelical movement in the Church of England from falling apart, and I dared to believe that my address was going to be crucial towards this end. I had been asked to set out a vision for the future of the Church of England. My hope was that, if the different factions which had developed within the Evangelical tradition could unite around that vision, we might be on the way to healing and cohesion.

Yet one must ask some big questions. How had we come to this? Why was it that the bishops in the Church who were identified as evangelicals had decided to call a national conference? How was it that in 1995, when the Evangelical tradition was numerically and proportionally stronger than it had ever been in the Church of England, its leaders felt so concerned? Before we can answer those questions, we must go back a long way and try to understand the tradition itself.

I was once asked to give a series of addresses in the Canterbury diocese on 'evangelical spirituality'. I began by making a few clarifications. Evangelicalism, I said, was not the same thing as fundamentalism (although fundamentalists would always describe themselves as evangelicals). Evangelicalism, I went on, was not the same thing as being charismatic – the spirituality often caricatured as 'happy-clappy'. Indeed, I argued, there was a sense that Evangelicalism was not the same thing as Protestantism. There were many Protestants who would not call themselves evangelical, and there was even a group in the Roman Catholic Church who liked to describe themselves as 'Evangelical Catholics'.

My audience in Canterbury appeared surprised at these words. No tradition in the Church is more misunderstood and more subjected to caricature than the Evangelical tradition. I added to their surprise by stating that the Evangelical tradition pre-dated the Anglo-Catholic, Liberal Catholic and Modernist traditions, thus making it the oldest tradition within the Church.

There are two defining strands, or 'bloodlines', within the Evangelical tradition. The first of these goes back to the

English Reformation and the minds of Cranmer, Ridley, Latimer and Tyndale, as well as the earlier Wycliffe. The second defining strand centres around the eighteenth-century Evangelical Awakening, led by such men as the Wesleys and Whitefield.

From our Reformation origins there is the great emphasis on the central role of the Bible as the ultimate arbiter of all matters of doctrine and practice. For evangelicals the Bible has this authority because it is to be viewed – as the Thirty-nine Articles put it – as 'God's word written'. Stripped of the political overlays, the English Reformation was about what things were 'necessary to salvation' and 'what was required of any man, that it should be believed as an article of faith' (Article 6). Over the centuries the Catholic Church, as an organization, had slipped into a position where it had itself become the authority with the power to decide these matters. The Bible was an unknown book to the congregations, and was even considered dangerous when put in the hands of the common people. William Tyndale was hunted throughout Europe, caught and executed simply for translating the Bible into English and getting it printed for widespread use. The English reformers, like their European counterparts, were essentially driven by a scholarly rediscovery of the New Testament.

Evangelical Anglicans are therefore Bible people to the core. They are also those who view the Church of England as a healthily reformed section of the Holy Catholic and Apostolic Church. They have never seen themselves as covert free church-men sheltering within the Church of England, but rather as the true heirs of that period in history when it reformed its doctrines and practices and formulated what we now call *The Book of Common Prayer*. Both the English Reformation and the later

Evangelical Awakening are firmly rooted in the history of the Church of England. Evangelicalism is indeed to be found in the Free Churches, and attractively so, but it is completely at home within Anglicanism.

If the Reformation rediscovered the proper authority for the Church, the Evangelical Awakening rediscovered its proper purpose – to witness widely to the good news of God. George Whitefield and John Wesley felt themselves driven to work outside existing Church structures in order to take the gospel to the unchurched masses of their own day. They saw that what went on inside the parish churches was only touching a very small section of the England that the Church was supposed to serve. John Wesley found preaching in the fields and marketplaces distasteful, but absolutely necessary.

As a teenager growing up in south London, I discovered that there was a raised area of my native Blackheath that was known as 'Whitefield's Mount'. It was there that the great evangelist would often preach to huge crowds, while local gentry ordered their carriages to be driven within range of the preacher's voice so that they could hear him from a safe distance. I remember one day going onto that low mount and standing in every conceivable preaching position, just to be able to say that I had stood where the great George Whitefield had taken his stand two centuries earlier.

While the Evangelical tradition has never dominated the Church, and has often been treated with disdain, it has always exhibited energy and creativity. In the nineteenth century it gave rise to more overseas and home missionary societies than any other section of the Church. Powerful evangelical laymen such as Wilberforce and Shaftesbury brought about great social changes affecting such matters as factory working conditions at home and the end of slavery in the colonies. The

Religious Tract Society (combining the efforts of Anglicans and Free Churchmen) sought to put Christian literature before the eyes of the masses at a time of growing literacy. Evangelical work among the students of the older universities produced an impressive string of Christian leaders whose impact was to be felt by generations to come.

Within the formal structures of the Church of England, however, the impact of Evangelicalism was never strong. The Anglo-Catholics and the Liberal Catholics became significantly more influential as the nineteenth century moved into the twentieth. The reaction of many evangelicals to the rediscovery of Catholic styles and practices was probably counterproductive. They tried to use the law to ban such growing practices as the reserved sacrament and mass vestments, and this may well have alienated many rank-and-file church members at the time.

Another reaction to developments, including scientific theories such as evolution, was that of opting out of debate. Evangelicals have often hidden behind the half-truth that all that matters is evangelism and holiness of life. Again and again they have pleaded these priorities and buried themselves in those agendas, leaving running the Church and grappling with modernity to others who were judged to be 'less spiritual'. It was fashionable in the 1930s for evangelicals to discourage their ordinands from studying theology at university level. It was felt that it might damage their faith.

When I was cutting my teeth as a teenage Christian, there were very few evangelicals in high office in the Church, and those who were found themselves viewed with suspicion. When Billy Graham came to London for his amazing 1954 'Greater London Crusade' he was publicly supported by only one bishop, a suffragan in the Chelmsford diocese.

It is true that the 1930s had seen the rise of a liberal version
of Evangelicalism, with some well-regarded clerics associated
with what was called the Anglican Evangelical Group
Movement. In the years following the war, however, the movement began to flag. Eventually, in 1967, it voted itself out of
existence.

While Anglican evangelicals had little say in the affairs of
the Church of England nationally, they made common cause
with Free Church evangelicals in such organizations as the
Evangelical Alliance, the Children's Special Service Mission
(later to become part of the Scripture Union) and the Inter
Varsity Fellowship, which worked powerfully among students. They had their own strong voluntary organizations
within the Anglican world. The two most significant of these
in the 1950s were the Church Pastoral Aid Society (CPAS)
and the Church Society. Both held patronage rights to hundreds of parishes. By appointing vicars and rectors to these
many parishes they kept evangelical witness alive throughout
England. They also promoted vigorous children's and youth
work in many parishes, and had funds that could be used to
help poorer parishes afford additional clergy and lay workers.

The truth was that, while evangelicals were politically weak
in the Church of the 1950s and 60s, their parish churches were
among the strongest and best attended. Again, because of
their great emphasis on children's and youth work, they began
producing a steady stream of ordination candidates, as well as
committed laypeople who would later move to parishes of
different theological hues and make their presence felt
through voluntary effort.

What was needed was leadership to arise within the tradition that was concerned to reconnect with the Church at large,
and which sought to bring evangelical insights and priorities

into the mainstream. By 1960 that leadership had clearly emerged in the person of John Stott, Rector of All Souls Church, Langham Place, in London. Unlike many evangelical leaders of the day, Stott was a well-equipped theologian, and young enough to be free of the largely defensive mind-sets of older generations within the tradition. He was also undeniably a pioneer in parish strategy, and led a congregation that was packing out a large central London church.

Stott grew up in the parish in which he was to serve his first and only curacy. He then became rector of the same parish, and even today is a member of the staff as rector emeritus. In his days as a schoolboy in Rugby, he had become a convinced and active Christian through the remarkable school work of the Reverend E. J. Nash – known to all his associates as 'Bash'. In the 1950s a remarkable group of young clerics emerged in the evangelical wing of the Church, and many of them were products of Nash's work – men like Michael Green, David Sheppard, John Collins and David Watson. Nash was concerned not only to bring schoolboys to faith but also to develop them as Christian leaders. Stott was soon involved in Christian leadership at his school and in Nash's summer camps. He was, in most ways, a typical product of evangelical work among public schools. His involvement in student work in, and later with, the Christian Unions was again typical of the products of Nash and others involved in similar work.

By the time I was ordained in 1960, Stott had founded the Eclectic Society. It was, in fact, the relaunching of a society that went back to the late eighteenth century and the ministry of the great hymn-writer John Newton. In its early days Newton's Eclectic Society was limited to some thirteen London clergy. They met 'for mutual intercourse and the investigation of spiritual truth'. Stott's later Eclectic Society was likewise limited to a small number of evangelical clergy, mostly those who had come from the same public school and 'Bash camp' background as himself. He set an upper age limit of forty – although this was somewhat elastic. The idea behind this was to provide a forum where younger evangelical clergy could feel free to discuss their understandings and perspectives free from the oversight of the older, and often more inflexible, evangelical leaders of the time. The first members tried to limit their numbers, and keep the enterprise at a modest level. It was soon clear, however, that many were wanting to join. It also became clear that Eclectics could well be an important influence throughout the Evangelical tradition, if not beyond. The first Eclectics decided to open their doors, and to open them wide.

The Eclectic Society rapidly expanded into regional groups, then began to hold national conferences with two hundred or more participants. This expansion ended the unintended but apparent public-school, closed-shop feel of the early days. Young evangelical clergymen of all backgrounds came together, but there was no doubting that the central guru of the movement was John Stott. His vision of an Evangelicalism that had intellectual integrity, that was prepared to think adventurously and that took the Church of England seriously characterized the whole movement.

Somewhere around 1963 I became a member, and it revolutionized my ministry. I joined a regional group and the annual conferences in the autumn became the highlight of my year. There was an absolute ferment of ideas in those early days, and some very significant things emerged from the study groups. From one came radical thinking about inner-city mission, with David Sheppard as the great driving force. From another came ideas and strategies for family services, with

Michael Botting prominent. From another came new music for youth work, with Michael Baughen, Norman Warren and Richard Bewes leading the way. Their work led to the successful publication of the two *Youth Praise* books. Norman Warren was also the author of the best-selling evangelistic tract of the century, *Journey into Life*.

It is worth noting that every one of the people just mentioned went on to perform significant roles in the national Church. Sheppard and Baughen became outstanding diocesan bishops, Warren became Archdeacon of Rochester, Bewes followed Baughen and Stott as Rector of All Souls, Langham Place, and Botting became an influential senior cleric in the Chester diocese. I do not believe there is a coincidence here. Eclectics bred leaders, and in this it reflected the mind-set of its creator, who was himself the product of an exceptional evangelist who bred leaders.

The Church at large hardly noticed the Eclectic Society in its early years. It would also be true to say that the vision of most members in those early years was focused on leading effective and growing parish churches rather than on central Church issues. Youth work, however, was taken very seriously by Eclectics, and one result of this was a steady flow of young ordinands from evangelical parishes. This guaranteed that the Evangelical tradition was going to have to be taken seriously. The Church at large was beginning to realize that the ordained ministry of future years would be increasingly dominated by those with evangelical perspectives.

Two things brought about a sea change in the relationship of the tradition with the Church of England as a whole. The first turning point was the first National Evangelical Anglican Congress, which was held at Keele University in 1967. In the two or three years of planning for the congress there was a remarkable shift of emphasis. The original plans had been for a thousand or so clergy and laypeople to gather from evangelical parishes and hear their key thinkers reading weighty papers. These papers would be available at the conference in a book, *Guidelines*, and each delegate would take home his or her copy for further reflection. In other words, it was to be a conference of a few participants and a large number of spectators.

As the congress planning entered its latter stages, however, the autumn Eclectics Conference of 1966 made it clear that its members were deeply uneasy about what was being proposed. There were late-night brainstorming sessions with people calling for more rank-and-file participation at the proposed congress. At that time I was working for the Church Pastoral Aid Society and was in charge of the publications related to the congress. I was therefore a member of the congress planning committee. I was also fully involved in the brainstorming sessions. It was not surprising that I ended up being charged by my fellow Eclectics to take their criticisms and suggestions to the main congress committee. John Stott's Young Turks were in revolt, and there were now too many of them to ignore.

I still remember the day I had to share these concerns with the congress committee. It was early winter, cold and snowing slightly. The meeting was in All Souls, Langham Place. It was only three or four months before the congress was due to take place. I was extremely nervous. I set out the concept of a more participative congress, where those attending would have read *Guidelines* before they came and would all engage in an exercise to produce a statement for publication. To my amazement, the whole committee welcomed every proposal. I discovered that they had all been feeling similar misgivings. It was agreed that an initial draft of the statement needed to be prepared, and I found myself on the drafting group.

The Keele Congress was a remarkable happening. Not only did Archbishop Ramsey think it important enough to accept an invitation to be the opening speaker, but the Church and national press was well represented. Every press report noted the vigour and vision of the assembly. While established leaders like John Stott and Jim Packer were inevitably significant participants, the ground-level drivers of the process were the younger Eclectics, with George Hoffman (later to found TEAR Fund) and Philip Crowe (later to be principal of Salisbury Theological College) acting as key co-ordinators. There were to be further congresses in 1977 and 1988, but while they had their merits they never recaptured the dramatic dynamism of 1967. And one of the main messages of the first congress was that evangelicals in the Church of England had to stop virtually being a church within a church. They had to play their part in the Church of England as a whole and see it as their home.

This encouragement to escape from self-imposed ghettos went further than the call to be more involved in the life and issues of the Church of England. A key paper at the congress was delivered by Professor Norman Anderson of London University. A leading layman in the Church Assembly, he spoke on issues relating to the Church's involvement in social and political matters. Victorian evangelicals such as Shaftesbury and Wilberforce had been in the van in such matters. Later evangelicals, however, had tended to regard this present world's affairs as a distraction from the central task of preparing people for the next. They left the pace to be set by those of a more liberal theological complexion, all of which reinforced evangelical disdain for the issues involved. Keele urged evangelicals to take social and political involvement more seriously. If it is true to say that God loves everybody, then the conditions in which people live, or are forced to live, must matter to him. If we are to say and mean the petition in the Lord's Prayer about God's will being 'done on earth as it is in heaven', then Christians cannot hide behind a totally next-world message.

The second turning point for evangelical participation in the Church of England came with the advent of synodical government in 1970. By that date the Keele mind-set had a stronger foothold in the evangelical constituency. With a new system of Church government coming into place, evangelicals were urged to stand through their network of Diocesan Evangelical Fellowships. The mode of election was to be by the single transferable vote system of proportional representation. This puzzled many at the time, but two Eclectics, Colin Buchanan and Peter Dawes (both later to become bishops), wrote a simple booklet explaining the system. They pointed out that one advantage was that, as long as people voted for those of their own tradition, the proportional representation system ensured that the vote could not be split and would settle at maximum strength behind a candidate of the preferred tradition.

Inevitably this politicized the synodical elections and thus the General Synod itself, but the politicization was already in existence from the old Church Assembly days. The only difference was that evangelicals were now becoming more streetwise.

They had not been without their champions in the old Church Assembly days – especially in the House of Laity. People like Sir Norman Anderson, Jack Wallace, Tony Kimpton, Harry Walker, Hugh Craig, Jill Dann and Gervase

Duffield were prominent evangelical spokespeople and had often exercised an influence beyond their numerical strength. It was the clergy who needed persuading to get involved, and by the early 1970s, through the efforts of people like Buchanan and Dawes, the challenge was beginning to be taken up.

General Synods are elected for a period of five years. By 1985, when I was elected, evangelicals had become very strong in the House of Laity and almost as well represented in the House of Clergy. There remained the matter of representation in the House of Bishops. Here entry to the Synod is not so easily responsive to strength in the parishes and deaneries. The House of Bishops contains every diocesan bishop, with a further ten places decided by an election among the suffragan bishops. No one becomes a diocesan bishop except by the choice of the prime minister, acting on specific advice from what is known as the Crown Appointments Commission. That commission takes widespread soundings and puts two names to the prime minister, who selects one and appoints on behalf of the Queen. Suffragans are the chosen colleagues of diocesan bishops (who have the suffrage in these matters, hence the term).

In the years leading up to 1980 there were very few bishops who could be clearly identified as coming from the evangelical stable. This was all the more surprising considering that at one stage in the 1970s both archbishops, Donald Coggan and Stuart Blanch, were rightly considered to be on the evangelical wing, as was John V. Taylor, who held the senior bishopric of Winchester. The composition of the General Synod's House of Bishops was, therefore, considerably out of tune with the other houses. David Sheppard had been made Suffragan Bishop of Woolwich in 1969. Maurice Wood (under whom Sheppard served his first curacy) had become Diocesan Bishop of Norwich in 1971. Sheppard went on to become the distinguished Bishop of Liverpool in 1975, but there seemed to be little change in evangelical strength on the bench of bishops until the 1980s.

In 1980 Timothy Dudley Smith, formerly General Secretary of the Church Pastoral Aid Society, became Suffragan Bishop of Thetford. Soon afterwards, John Taylor was made Diocesan Bishop of St Albans. That began a steady trickle of episcopal appointments. In 1982 Michael Baughen was appointed Bishop of Chester, Michael Whinney went to Aston and, later, Southwell (where ill health cut short what could have been a fine ministry). Bill Persson went to Doncaster, Colin Scott to Hulme, Jim Roxburgh to Barking, George Carey to Bath and Wells in 1987, with Peter Dawes to Derby and Michael Turnbull to Rochester a year later. Other evangelicals became bishops fairly steadily through the 1990s, until we reached the situation at the turn of the century in which nearly thirty of the serving bishops in the Church of England could be described as evangelical – not far short of a third of the total number.

The Church enters the twenty-first century with a strong contingent of evangelicals on the bench of bishops, a growing percentage of evangelical men and now women serving as parish priests, and with evangelical laypeople in the majority in the House of Laity of the General Synod. Over half of those in residential training for the ordained ministry have chosen to go to the evangelical colleges. Once again we must ask, why was a conference called in 1995 to deal with a perceived crisis in this apparently flourishing tradition?

To answer this we must look at two developments in recent history. The first is related to what was started in the Keele

Congress, but the second comes from a totally different quarter. These developments effectively ended the influence of John Stott on contemporary Anglican Evangelicalism.

Keele marked the end of the tradition's defensiveness. It sensed its numerical strength within the Church and noted that it was beginning to meet with some respect. Evangelical clergy, as we have seen, began to catch up with their laity in taking Church politics seriously. People began to make themselves available to serve on diocesan committees. They began to move into dialogue as opposed to confrontation. They began to listen more. They began to see the strength of other positions. They had to learn, in synodical settings, to settle for less than they preferred as opposed to getting absolutely nothing. In short, they began to lose the uniting effect of feeling like a persecuted minority.

All this was happening at a time when the ever-growing number of evangelical clergy meant that there were simply not enough long-standing evangelical churches available to them. They had to accept appointments in non-evangelical parishes. Most of them went into such ministries with sensitivity towards the way things had been conducted in the past. Thus the distinctive surplice and scarf robing of evangelical clergy in the past changed to the use of coloured stoles in many cases. There was also a strong tendency at the time – and Keele specifically encouraged this – to move towards the Eucharist being the main service on Sundays. At the same time, the national Church was introducing the 'Series 2' and 'Series 3' experimental forms of service, and 'westward position' was becoming the norm. Westward position was to do with the stance that the celebrant (or 'president' as he was increasingly being described) took while conducting a Communion service. *The Book of Common Prayer* had revealed its

Reformation roots by placing the celebrant at the north side of the table. This unique idea was a reaction to the priest standing in front of the table or altar with his back to the people in a way that could be interpreted as making him an intermediary.

During the nineteenth century and into the twentieth, most churches had reverted to the pre-Reformation eastward position, with the priest in front of the Communion table. Evangelicals persisted with north side and the Church Pastoral Aid Society, in making grants to parishes to help pay curates, made north side a condition of their grants. The move to westward, where the celebrant was behind the table and facing the congregation, put evangelicals in a quandary. Their arguments against eastward seemed to be met almost as much with westward position as with north side. An almost total reorientation took place over a period of ten years.

All this may seem fussy and of little significance, but the cumulative effect of these changes in attire and practice was that evangelicals lost several of their long-standing distinguishing marks. They were visually becoming absorbed into the mainstream Church of England.

This ending of defensiveness and distinctiveness did not stop with liturgical practices. Evangelicals were increasingly taking theological study seriously, and numbers were entering the academic sphere. Holding predictable party lines did not easily square with coming at questions in a scholarly fashion. In particular, the study of hermeneutics (which deals with how we read and interpret the Bible) became a key question. Evangelicals held strong views as to the inspiration of Scripture and its trustworthiness in matters of faith and doctrine. The phrase 'the Bible says' was frequently used and was supposed to settle any argument there and then.

To say 'the Bible says' begs several questions, however. What do we mean by 'Bible'? In one sense there is no such thing as 'Bible'. The Bible is, in fact, a term we use to cover a whole library of books, of differing types of literary character, written over hundreds of years, by people living in very different cultures from our own. Again, a study of the different Gospels, and the different writers of the epistles, reveals differing emphases and the clear signs of being addressed to different readerships.

Evangelicalism was producing its scholars and they were beginning to point out that the Bible was not quite such a simple book as the tradition made it out to be. If one was to interpret the Bible for today's reader, one had to be clear as to the culture and circumstances of the original readers, as well as the culture and mind-set of the original writers. Yes, it may well be true that the Bible is God's word written, but the writing was done by fallible men who were the products of their age and culture.

What this meant was that evangelicals began to see those of their own kind talking more cautiously and tentatively where once all had seemed to be reassuringly certain. The tradition had long believed in the value of 'proof texts' – single verses from the Bible that clarified and settled doctrinal points. Now they were being told that proof texts were not always helpful. They often needed to be balanced by other texts, and they always needed to be understood in the light of the particular circumstances of the time when they were first written.

The second National Evangelical Anglican Congress in 1977 is often cited as the time when hermeneutics escaped from the academic classroom and collided with rank-and-file parishioners. It was not an easy meeting and the reaction of many to this, and to some other views that were being voiced, was to brand it as evidence of 'liberalism' creeping in to pollute the truth.

Timothy Dudley Smith, in his biography of John Stott, mentions a letter that Stott had written shortly after NEAC2. He had received a letter from the Archbishop of Sydney, Sir Marcus Loane, who had heard that some disturbing trends were surfacing among younger evangelicals. Stott admitted in reply that he had seen at the congress 'disturbing signs . . . of the beginnings of a new "liberal evangelicalism"'. In fact, the term 'liberal evangelical', reminiscent of those associated with the old Anglican Evangelical Group Movement, has never resurfaced. What has emerged in the years since NEAC2, however, is the term 'open evangelical', which has become increasingly used in recent years.

I remain somewhat bemused by the term and how it emerged. I am not aware of any defining doctrinal positions which mark out whether one is 'open' or 'conservative'. One is left feeling that it is more to do with atmospheric matters such as sensitivity, and a readiness to work alongside those of other traditions in the Church of England as it is. Some day someone will explain it all to me, and I will be pleased to find out, because I find that I have myself been identified as someone who is of the 'open' variety!

The hermeneutics issue which came to light at NEAC2 is something to which we must return. More than anything, it lay behind the serious fracture that the 1995 conference in Westminster Chapel was seeking to heal. That fracture was not about hermeneutics in itself, but about the way it applied to a specific issue, namely the ordination of women to the priesthood. We need, however, to backtrack and consider the second development in recent history that ended the influence of John Stott on the Evangelical movement.

In the early 1960s – during my second curacy – a new talking point was beginning to surface. It centred around such phrases as 'the baptism of the Holy Spirit' and 'speaking in tongues'. These were not new phrases or themes. They relate to material that can be found in the New Testament, and they came into prominence in the Christian world at the beginning of the twentieth century in the form of the Pentecostal movement. In my youth fellowship and student days I was vaguely aware of Pentecostalism. It seemed to me to be a fringe brand of evangelical Christianity exemplified in such denominations as the Assemblies of God and the Elim Pentecostal Church. What happened in the 1960s, however, was different. From within the older and major denominations, people were claiming Pentecostal experiences. Even the Roman Catholics were experiencing this charismatic awakening.

An American book began to do the rounds. It was called *The Cross and the Switchblade*. It told the remarkable story of its author, David Wilkerson, who led a ministry among young drug addicts in the USA. Wilkerson belonged to one of the long-established Pentecostal denominations, but his book was being read by people in mainstream churches. Wilkerson spoke about addicts being healed miraculously, being baptized in the Spirit and speaking in tongues. Christian bookshops often stocked the book, and others like it, under the counter, fearful of putting it on display, but sales boomed. People were beginning to ask questions of their own spiritualities in the light of the book's challenge, and evangelicals found themselves particularly put to the test.

What Wilkerson's book did was to make its readers ask whether their biblical mind-set was truly biblical. Did it, for instance, have a place for a God who acted in power? Did it have a place for healing, for direct revelations and contemporary words of prophecy? Had twentieth-century Christians, including evangelicals, rationalized away miracles as a present-day possibility? Above all, were we refusing to face up to what the New Testament appeared to suggest, which was that every person needs an experiential baptizing in the Holy Spirit similar to that which came on the apostles on the Day of Pentecost?

Gradually, what became known as 'the charismatic movement' began to gather pace. Two of John Stott's curates, Michael Harper and John Collins, emerged among the leaders of this movement. This was fascinating, because Stott himself had deep reservations about the whole issue. Harper helped to found the Fountain Trust and became its first director. This was a very brave thing to do, because the Evangelical movement in the 1960s was cool, if not hostile. There were good reasons for such coolness. Evangelicalism has always suffered from holiness movements which tended to prey on those already converted, suggesting that they needed more than their basic faith in Christ. Again, holiness movements had a track record of splitting congregations, and it was not long before this tendency appeared to be happening as a result of the new emphasis on spiritual gifts and the need for baptism in the Holy Spirit.

The emphasis on experiences is always disturbing. The traditional evangelical way of imparting assurance was to point to the promises of Scripture and urge the believer to trust in a God who keeps his word. What charismatics seemed to be saying was that one needed to know from experience that the Holy Spirit had entered one's life and that – some said – the proof of this was 'speaking in tongues'. All this, it was claimed, was merely a replication of what happened on the first Day of Pentecost recorded in Acts 2.

The problem here is threefold. First, there are those who desperately want to have this experience, but it does not seem to happen for them. What does that say about their standing with God? Second, there is always the danger that a subtle counterfeiting and self-delusion can take place, which might lead to later disillusion. Third, how can anybody be sure that what the New Testament describes as 'speaking in tongues' has any relationship to what people are practising in contemporary charismatic spirituality? There are no reassuring objective benchmarks to measure subjective experiences. Nobody who was there at the Day of Pentecost is here now to vouch for their authenticity. The very thing that is supposed to generate assurance contains the seeds of uncertainty.

By the early 1970s the charismatic renewal was the biggest thing affecting the evangelicals. The tradition was divided into two camps over the issue, and sometimes both camps were represented within one congregation. Reaction from some clergy to these new emphases led to breakaway congregations being formed. Significant cultural differences marked out the two camps. Charismatic worship stimulated a wave of new worship songs which were strong on emotion and less so on doctrine. Many of these songs – and some were particularly haunting – focused not on the one worshipped but on the one doing the worship. They suggested what the singer should be doing or feeling. Lines such as 'I lift my hands', accompanied by a melodic surge, were obviously intended to bring about exactly that physical response.

Whole congregations would be encouraged to stand and sing choruses repeatedly, raising their hands and even dancing in the emotion of self-offering to a loving Father. Particularly haunting were those times when free 'singing in tongues' would take place. For many this was a much needed release from the more cerebral, word-centred worship that marked traditional evangelical worship and the Prayer Book. Others, however, could not cope with such demonstrative moments in church. The English parish church, rightly or wrongly, has long been a place where a worshipper could remain private in public. To such people, the effects of the charismatic renewal were emotionally tyrannical.

For a community church – as opposed to a gathered congregation – this is a critical matter. The Church of England has long exercised a sort of chaplaincy relationship with the people of its parishes. It has, in effect, said, 'We are here when you want us. You can come and go, and you can travel at your own pace.' What the renewal culture does is virtually to insist that the worshipper is part of the whole body of believers and joins in whatever mood is being created by the leadership.

There were, therefore, particular problems for the Church of England – and evangelicals within it – with this new renewal culture. It must also be said, however, that there were also many real gains. Charismatic worship does not allow the worshipper to be cool about God. While for some there may be an emotional intrusion here, there is also surely a proper challenge. Why is it appropriate to shout and get excited at a football match, but not so when it comes to singing the praises of a loving Father and a brave Saviour? Why is it so obviously a criticism to describe a church as 'happy-clappy'? Is there something so obviously virtuous about being solemn or gloomy? Did not Jesus suggest that when the 'Bridegroom' was present it was appropriate to rejoice? Again, are we not supposed to believe that Jesus is alive by his Spirit and that he can make things happen? What is the point of intercessory prayer if God is denied the power to act in response? And when people criticize the charismatic movement as too emotional, is it not the truth that it has helped many people to become whole, with their feelings being reconnected to their minds?

Like many, I found myself both critical and yet positively affected by the changes brought in by the charismatic renewal. One of its great positives was that it opened up new lines of fellowship between Protestants and Roman Catholics. It would need a book in itself to do justice to all the issues involved. My purpose here, however, is to focus on some aspects of the renewal that had great significance for the sort of Evangelicalism that was characterized by Stott, Eclectics and NEAC1.

First, the charismatic emphases inevitably affected the place of the Bible in worship and in the discernment of God's will. The strong emphasis on a God who does things *now* contrasts with a God who did things *then* and can be read about later. This means that the believer is encouraged to expect 'words from the Lord' either in his or her own experience, or through others in the congregation. Guidance is less about reading what God is like, and what Jesus did in similar situations, and making deductions and applications. It is more about what you feel God is saying to you in the present. When our final authority becomes what we feel God is saying, the place of the Bible is at least challenged. On the other hand, there have always been stories of people who did remarkable things as a result of feeling directly addressed by the Holy Spirit.

There were two other effects of the charismatic renewal that ran contrary to the Evangelicalism of Stott, Eclectics and NEAC1. Renewal, by definition, turns one's gaze upon oneself, or one's congregation, to face the need for improvement and change. The danger here is that this can mean a switch of focus from outward to inward. One of the defining marks of Evangelicalism is the Wesley-like desire to look beyond the congregation to those who have not yet discovered the gospel of Christ. The renewal movement could sometimes have the effect of making leadership structures, congregational relationships and worshipping styles more important and time-consuming than anything else. This was not always the case. Probably the most influential leader of the charismatic movement in the 1970s was David Watson, who was also the outstanding evangelist of his day. It also has to be noted that the remarkable Alpha Course originated in a strongly charismatic church and became one of the most used evangelistic approaches in British churches during the 1990s.

The second effect of this inward preoccupation was that the affairs of the Church of England at large became less important. There were new networks and alliances for the charismatic congregation, often focused on large inter-denominational conventions such as Spring Harvest and New Wine.

When the time came, in 1988, for a third National Evangelical Anglican Congress, a very different constituency existed. It had become fragmented, with the different groups looking in different directions for their leadership. In 1986 I was asked to be the chairman for the congress. The congress was convened by the Church of England Evangelical Council, who selected all the people on the planning committee and virtually gave us terms of reference. We were to plan a different sort of gathering from the congresses of 1967 and 1977. It was to be more celebratory in tone, like the very successful annual Spring Harvest conventions. It was to offer a large range of workshops and seminars, turning attenders into students rather than participants. And because of this, and because of the differences within the tradition, it was not to think of drafting any statement to the outside world.

I will always regret accepting these terms of reference for NEAC3. I was asked to chair both the planning committee and a reference group. I found myself out of step with the underlying philosophy of the congress (or 'celebration' as it was to be called), and after a short time I resigned from the planning group and simply remained on the less influential reference group. I should have stayed and fought for a different vision. NEAC3 drew a respectable number of participants and provided them with plenty of training opportunities, but it was soon written off as a failure. It also revealed divisions on some of the most important areas of evangelical belief, such as the nature of the gospel itself. It was a diversion rather than a landmark, and I will always feel that much of the blame for this rests with me.

And so to Westminster Chapel and January 1995. The remarkable thing about this conference was that it was called by a group of bishops and others in senior positions within the Church – all of whom were proud to be called evangelical. The key player was Michael Baughen, the Bishop of Chester and formerly the man who succeeded John Stott as Rector of All Souls, Langham Place.

Baughen and his colleagues were increasingly disturbed by the divisions within the evangelical constituency. They were coming to light at the very time when the tradition was becoming strong enough to be the supreme shaping influence on the national Church. The great concern was not about the charismatic evangelicals. To their credit, they were characterized with a certain inclusive graciousness. They may have had their preferred alliances, but they never sought to oppose other evangelicals who held different priorities. The group that drew forth the concerns of the conference organizers was the group that had given rise to an organization calling itself 'Reform'. The issue that, more than anything, gave rise to Reform was the ordination of women to the priesthood.

Reform was only one manifestation of a growing anxiety, felt by many evangelicals, about the way things were going in the central affairs of the Church of England. In spite of much greater evangelical involvement in the structures, it was felt that too much was being conceded to a liberal theological mind-set. Many evangelical clergy and laity could not believe what their friends and former colleagues seemed to be saying in the debates that led up to the decision to ordain women to the priesthood. Surely, they felt, Scripture was absolutely clear on the matter.

There were clear scriptural texts which prohibited women speaking in church, or so it was felt. There were passages that, at face value, pointed to male headship in the divine ordering of things. The very creation narratives stressed the primacy of the male, with the woman as 'helpmeet'. Again there was, it was argued, no evidence that women were among Christ's apostles or the leadership of the New Testament Church. When the new hermeneutics were deployed to point up cultural and contingent reasons for some of these texts, this simply seemed to be a case of manipulating the truth of Scripture.

It would be wrong to see this as an anti-women sentiment. One evangelical clergyman I know said that he deeply wished that Scripture supported the ordination of women because he would like to see it. The problem was that his conscience would not let him support disobedience to the revealed word of God. The issue was not women's ministry, it was the authority of Scripture. Lurking behind this concern was the suspicion that more disobedience was to follow. If Scripture could be bent to support the ordination of women, could it not just as easily be made to support the recognition of gay marriages and the ordination of practising homosexuals?

There were strong voices in the new Reform movement who were calling for financial sanctions. Evangelical congregations were often the biggest and therefore the wealthiest congregations throughout the dioceses. As such, they were close to being the paymasters of the other traditions through the diocesan quota system. Why, people began to say, should they pay money into a central kitty to finance churches led by those who did not believe basic credal doctrines? Why should evangelical congregations be taxed to finance liberal parishes and clergy who made no effort to share the gospel in their neighbourhoods?

Again, the anxiety felt by evangelical congregations at perceived trends towards the legitimization of homosexual practices in the Church led to other moves. Some churches wanted to check where any particular bishop stood on this issue before he could come to conduct a confirmation. There were even some freelance, ex-missionary bishops who were considered 'clean' on the matter, and who were ready to come in to confirm in sensitive parishes.

When that was added to the large number of evangelical parishes – often charismatic in colour – who expressed little concern for the structures of the Church and left leadership to others, Michael Baughen and his friends felt that the evangelical bishops had to stand up and be counted. Every keynote speaker at the conference was a bishop, and it was hoped that they would commend themselves in such a way that there would be a restoration of confidence in their leadership and theological soundness.

The conference was packed out. The venue had been changed to Westminster Chapel to make room for a greater attendance than originally expected. On the Saturday morning I stood up to deliver my address. I argued that the Elizabethan Settlement had given us a Church that was meant to be *for* England rather than of it. I argued that from the first there had always been diversity of opinion within the Church, but that unity was maintained by a common recognition of the need to serve the people of the country. I tried to set out that it could not be a Church that only represented one group or insight, and that our mission was to work together to serve the whole country rather than to lock ourselves into narrow parochialism. I spoke about the great evangelistic challenges posed by a complicated web of cultures in present-day society. I ended with a strong plea to reach out to children with the gospel.

> I am convinced that we have two main tasks in evangelism. To share the faith with our own generation and to keep the faith for the next generation.
>
> The older I get, the more I see that I am a Christian because people down the centuries have passed on the faith from one generation to another. Now it is our turn. You and I have been entrusted with the gospel by a God who measures time in centuries rather than seconds. That is why the future spiritual health of our country must matter to us . . .

The years have rolled on since the Westminster Conference. Things are little different. The tradition remains divided, although the rhetoric is gentler.

The problem for today's evangelicals relates directly to our numerical strength. We are no longer a minority united by a sense of being undervalued. We are no longer able to spell out, from a distance, simple solutions to the problems facing a complex voluntary organization. We are part of the coalition trying to lead the Church of England as it really is, warts and all, in very complicated times. I do not believe that the differences within the tradition are essentially doctrinal. They are to do with our different perceptions of the reality that confronts us. Are we outsiders waiting for changes before we fully identify, or are we insiders working patiently for those changes? I would argue that the sixteenth-century reformers were of the latter mind-set and that we should follow their example.

One thing seems clear. Because of the steady flow of ordinands from evangelical parishes, the Church of England will become increasingly staffed by evangelical clergy over the next twenty years. It is very likely that it will be dominated by Evangelicalism. Whether that will make it more united is another matter. The irony is that because of the tendency of some to suspect those in structural leadership, the practice of many to bury themselves in their parishes and the preference of others to make their alliances in inter-denominational settings, the future may give us a largely evangelical Church of England with much of its senior leadership in the hands of those from the other traditions.

8

Trumpeting the Voluntary

The letter inviting me to consider working for the Church
Pastoral Aid Society (CPAS) was handwritten on a memo slip
measuring four inches by six. It was dated the 9th November
1965. It was signed by the secretary of the Society, Timothy
Dudley Smith. It began:

> My Dear Gavin
>   I wonder if you would be willing to come to central London one
> day soon and talk about the possibility of joining us at Falcon
> Court to take up the (newly created) post of Publications
> Secretary.

At the time I was the minister of St John and St Matthew,
South Hornchurch, in riverside Essex. I had started as the
curate attached to the church, which was a daughter church in
the parish of Rainham. While I was there, a decision was
made to start working for the daughter church to become a
parish in its own right, and I was put on the same pay scale as
an incumbent and encouraged to feel something more than a
mere curate.

There was, therefore, plenty of incentive to stay. I remember that 1965 was the year when the Church of England seemed to wake up to my existence. The little letter from CPAS was the fourth invitation to have come my way that year, and I found it the most compelling.

I had first heard of CPAS as a boy in Blackheath. I was somewhere around twelve when an invitation came to have tea with a certain Miss Barton. She lived in a large house by the heath and was often to be seen riding her bicycle, armed with a tennis racket, on her way to the courts. She was a triumphant survivor of a more genteel age who was well loved in our church. When I turned up along with several other children of my age, a maid served us with orange squash and biscuits.

I do not think that we knew beforehand why we had been invited, but we soon found out. Miss Barton had set up a slide projector and she was going to tell us about the camps run by CPAS for 'poor children from the cities'. As the black-and-white photographic slides were projected onto a screen, I remember being captivated by the scenes of fun and games at a campsite in Burstow, near what is now Gatwick Airport. Far from being 'poor' children, I thought they were very lucky ones. Miss Barton told us that the camps were only a part of the important work that this evangelical society conducted to assist our parish churches with mission in our own country. I went home clutching a collecting box and with a child's conviction that these camps were important, and that they looked jolly good fun!

Some six years later, I found myself helping at one of those very camps – and the site was Burstow. The boys (about forty or fifty of them) slept in a large wooden hut, while the 'officers' slept in bell tents nearby. At one end of the hut was a dining area and the cookhouse was set nearby, relying on a wood-fuelled range.

The Society became important to me a few years after that, when I was contemplating my ordination training. It awarded me a grant to help with the costs. In return I was expected to attend an annual residential conference, which was good quality and therefore no penance. When the time came for me to be ordained, I was sent to a parish that could not afford a curate's stipend. Once again, the Society was there to help. As with hundreds of other new curates at that time, my employment was only possible because of a grant from CPAS.

Many years later, I received a letter offering me a parish in a university city. The patronage for the appointment was held by CPAS. To this day, the Society holds the right of appointment to hundreds of English parishes and is a key player in clergy movements.

Every grant-aided curate was expected to undertake a number of deputation sermons on behalf of the Society. One of the outcomes of all this was that generations of evangelical clergymen felt indebted to the Society, knew its work well, and tended to hold it in warm regard. They also realized that the Society could hold the keys to future jobs because of its large amount of patronage. It was a very powerful organization.

It is important to realize that in the first half of the twentieth century, CPAS was a major flag-carrier for the evangelical cause in the Church of England. When there was a strong chance in 1928 that the Church of England would introduce a revised Prayer Book, which was perceived to move worship in a more Catholic direction, CPAS was prominent in rallying opposition. The House of Commons was vigorously lobbied and the new book did not gain the parliamentary approval that was necessary for its legal use in the established Church. While the Society claimed that its overriding concern was mission, it unashamedly took the line that the promotion of Evangelicalism was necessary if effective mission was to go forward.

When I was training for the ministry, the Church of England was 'them', and organizations like CPAS and Church Society were 'us'. Other key standard-bearers in the Church were the missionary societies like the Church Missionary Society, the Bible Churchman's Missionary Society and the South American Missionary Society. It is no exaggeration to say that evangelical clergy and congregations were more focused around these 'voluntary societies' than they were around the official structures of the Church. They were re-assuring focal points in the middle of a sprawling national Church that was seen to be dominated by Anglo-Catholicism and liberalism. They were defining points. It was quite common to see an advertisement in the Church press for an organist to work in a church which described itself as 'CPAS/CMS' or 'CPAS/BCMS'.

A friend of mine once told me of an exchange that took place between him and a diocesan bishop in the 1960s. The bishop complained that evangelicals were really an empire within an empire. He complained that evangelical clergy looked far too much to agencies like CPAS and Church Society for their appointments rather than to the bishops. My friend's gracious but firm response was to remind the bishop that in diocese after diocese the story was that bishops 'seemed very happy to license evangelicals to battle in front-line parishes, but were less willing to invite them into "the officers' mess"'!

When that small, handwritten slip of paper came onto my

desk from CPAS in November 1965 (I still have it), it was doing far more than asking me to consider a job. It was inviting me to consider joining an élite and powerful group within the Evangelical Anglican scene. The offices in Falcon Court, off London's Fleet Street, were seen by many of us to be the virtual headquarters of the Evangelical movement in the Church of England.

Voluntary societies have always played an important, and yet ambiguous, part in the life of the Church. It may surprise many to be told that there is no official Church of England training college, and that there is no official Church of England missionary agency. History bestowed on England a Church which was a loosely co-ordinated number of dioceses with very little by way of central organization. The entire focus of every diocese, until comparatively recently, was inwards towards its own parishes. The training colleges and the missionary agencies (whether they be for home or overseas mission) were all dreamed up by entrepreneurial groups, mostly in the nineteenth century, and mostly with theological axes to grind.

While evangelicals were active in creating these parachurch voluntary societies, the Catholic wing also generated its societies. The Additional Curates Society, for example, engaged in a similar ministry to CPAS regarding funding places for newly ordained clergy. The United Society for the Propagation of the Gospel (USPG, formerly SPG) could claim to be older than any of the evangelical mission agencies. There were also societies that embraced all the traditions, such as the Mothers' Union and the Church Army, while other agencies like the British and Foreign Bible Society were inter-denominational.

The *Church of England Year Book* lists a bewildering array

of such societies, which includes the two Church newspapers, both totally clear of official editorial control. As many of these societies control very significant areas of ministry, it all makes for a very confusing picture. The bishops and archbishops of the Church of England have little control of key areas of the Church's life. The training colleges that prepare the clergy for their future ministries, the right to appoint clergy to hundreds of parishes and the main organs of internal communication are all in private hands.

More than half my years in the ministry were spent on the staff of the Church Pastoral Aid Society. I spent five years publishing books, booklets and film strips for use in the parishes. I left to work in another publishing concern for three years, then returned to serve the Society as Secretary for Evangelism for a further eighteen years. During that time I saw many changes. I also saw the Society lose a great deal of its power. As Evangelicalism grew and, in the spirit of the Keele Congress, threw itself increasingly into the main structures of the Church, the need for its own supportive structures fell away.

The biggest change, however, had nothing to do with the growth of Evangelicalism. It had everything to do with new financial realities in the dioceses. During the 1960s and 70s the Church got a grip on its strange ways of funding clergy. When my elder brother was appointed in 1960 to be the incumbent of two rural parishes, some of his pay came in rents from glebeland. He had to balance being a pastor to all his people and a landowner to some of them. Across the country there was a strange array of endowments that meant that some parishes carried a relatively high stipend, while others offered much smaller remuneration. All this changed over about ten to fifteen years. Glebeland funding was centralized and shared out on a more equitable basis. Gradually dioceses got their act together regarding the stipends of incumbents, and the same mind-set began to apply to assistant curates. It was not long before the funding of ordinands in training was also handled on a more centralized basis.

What this meant was that CPAS lost a great deal of influence and power. Along with the Church Society, it was no longer needed as an alternative support structure for evangelical clergy, working in a Church they often found alien to their vision. The Society could no longer play the money card which made it possible for curates to work in needy parishes. The dioceses had taken up these responsibilities, and it is hard to argue that this was not a proper thing for them to do.

My years in the Society, especially in my second role as an advisor and co-ordinator for local church evangelism, were years when the Society was in transition. The only two traditional ministries that were still significant were those of advising and seeking out ordinands (something the Society was doing before Church House Westminster took up the challenge) and patronage.

Patronage, however, was becoming a more complicated and compromised area of activity. As the Church began to feel the effects of dwindling clergy numbers, it armed itself with powers under the Pastoral Measure which allowed it to suspend the right of a patron to appoint. This would be brought into play when, for example, the bishop felt that two or more parishes needed to be brought together under the leadership of one priest. Such moves from bishops could be contested, but while patrons had vested interests in terms of the preservation of a particular churchmanship, they had to accept that there were simply too few clergy to spread around as in past times.

The longer I worked for CPAS, the more I felt that we were running on a large reservoir of goodwill from former times and those supporters who could remember them. If we were to survive, however, we had to be seen to be offering services that clearly met pastoral and evangelistic needs of the parish churches in the new era. Two developments in the 1970s helped in this regard.

The first was the development in 1974 of a Department for Evangelism, which I was asked to lead. We were able to offer advice and consultancy, and also staff evangelists to take missions and other sorts of evangelistic projects. As the years moved on, we experimented with something that was an echo of our earlier ministry. We funded urban evangelists to work in attachment to inner-city parishes. Such churches had little use for one-week preaching projects. What they needed was an extra member of staff with evangelistic gifts, working for up to three years at a time. This development required big financial grants, and we could only fund a few. It was never easy to find ideal people with the gifts and the willingness to engage in this sort of ministry. Not every appointment worked well, but a few did. Interestingly, most of those lay evangelists who worked on the scheme ended up getting ordained!

The second development was something that caught me by surprise. In 1975 the Church Society handed over the control of its youth and children's ministries to CPAS. This meant that CPAS now controlled the largest youth organizations working in the Church of England. Hundreds of churches were affiliated to the Church Youth Fellowships Association and to the larger Pathfinders and Explorers Bible class organizations. To these were added Climbers and Scramblers for the very young. Why Church Society passed over these parts of its work, I shall never know. I think it proved to be the end of the real contribution of that Society to the work of the Church. It was, however, a stroke of very good fortune for my organization.

As these two new areas of ministry were developing and increasingly characterizing the work of CPAS, the publishing department began to run into serious troubles. When I started my work in that department in 1966, it was a small and clearly focused operation. We were producing material that could be sold at the back of churches and used in the everyday life of the clergy and congregations. We knew from our unique relationship with the evangelical parishes exactly where there were gaps in what was provided by the relatively few publishers specializing in Christian literature. The problem is that one cannot stand still in any commercial operation, and inasmuch as we had to cover costs, pay staff and earn our keep within the Society, we were indeed a commercial operation. I tried to enlarge our range of publications, targeting the specialist Christian bookshops as much as the church bookstalls.

At the very time I started, CPAS had just launched a new song book for Christian youth groups called *Youth Praise*. It was put together by a group mainly composed of enthusiastic younger clergy, who were wrestling with the datedness of what they were asking their youth groups to sing. Most of the group met up through their involvement in Eclectics. Timothy Dudley Smith, who developed the new publishing department before my arrival, took an enormous gamble in offering to publish the work of this group. Music publishing is a very specialized area. There were plenty of snags along the way.

In 1966 the book was published. It was an instant success, requiring an immediate reprint, and then another. Although I was able to produce a few other big-selling publications, nothing rivalled the sales of *Youth Praise*. Soon we were pre-

paring *Youth Praise 2*. Extra staff and extra storage were
needed. As I learned more about publishing, I discovered that
the worst thing that can happen to a small publisher is to have
a best-seller! Unless there is great wisdom and expertise, what
happens is that you tool up for a level of sales that, in the end,
you cannot maintain.

In due course, people began to look in other directions for
popular church music. The charismatic movement was characterized by a new type of worship song, and as the movement
spread so did the demand for books of such songs. *Youth
Praise* passed out of fashion less than ten years after its introduction. People rightly perceived a different sub-theology
reflected in its material. Books like *The Sound of Living
Waters* replaced it, and as they did, the CPAS publishing
department began to creak badly.

I was out of the publishing side well before this, but I think
that some of my decisions led to the department's eventual
downfall. In 1971 I accepted an invitation to move to the
Lutterworth Press. I felt that this publishing house (owned by
another voluntary society) was better placed for me to
develop into a wider sphere of religious publishing. I needed
a new challenge. In the event, I returned to CPAS after only
three years. It was at Lutterworth, however, that I saw more
clearly what was happening in the whole area of Christian
publishing. I also saw why things were going to get harder for
CPAS.

What was happening in the years between 1965 and 1975
was an explosion of commercial publishing targeting the
Christian readership. Before 1965 there were relatively few
publishing houses in this field. Some, like Inter-Varsity Press,
had a very clearly defined market – in their case, the Christian
Unions in the universities and colleges. Others, like Hodder

& Stoughton and Collins, were top-rank secular publishing houses that carried a religious list. In the mid-1960s Edward England, an experienced Christian bookshop executive, went to Hodders to become the religious books editor. He made a huge impact on the whole scene. He and his company brought tremendous professionalism and significant investment into what had been a rather modest field of operations. Collins and the other publishers felt they had to respond. American evangelical publishers, who were used to selling into their own large markets, began to open up imprints in the United Kingdom. Attempts were made to improve the professionalism of the specialist bookshops and, for a while, the market expanded to a remarkable degree.

By the end of the 1970s, however, the market was beginning to show signs of saturation. While more and more books were projected at Christians, the numbers in our congregations were, in fact, declining. Something was going to snap, and the CPAS publishing department (known as Falcon Books) came to grief in 1978, with others to follow over the next decade.

I enjoyed publishing, but I became increasingly concerned at what was happening. My motivation for taking the CPAS job in 1966 was that of finding new ways to communicate the gospel to new groups of people. What I found I was doing, at both CPAS and Lutterworth, was targeting existing groups of Christians and trying to make them buy material that would only be of significance to them, and of no significance whatsoever to those outside our churches.

I came to feel that the evangelical publishing houses were increasingly becoming a component within a closed culture. It was a closed culture within society, and even a closed culture within the Church. As I looked at what was developing in the

1970s, and has indeed continued to develop, I felt I was seeing a sort of all-enveloping entertainment industry for Christians. If they wanted to, they could read only Christian books, listen only to Christian records, tapes and CDs, go only on Christian holidays and even only be entertained by Christian entertainers.

It was very difficult to break new ground and to launch new authors. The commercial considerations became paramount. Thus an established and popular author, saying the same thing again with some slight new angle, was always preferred before an unknown with something new to say. The taste of those in the marketplace dictated editorial policy. It also – understandably – governed what the Christian bookshops would stock. For example, it was very difficult to get a book in favour of the charismatic movement into the shops before 1965, and it was equally difficult to get a book that was critical of the movement into the shops in 1975.

By 1980 CPAS had closed its publishing department, and there was no shortage of pain at the end. Today the Society still produces publications, but they take the form of resource material aimed particularly at Christian workers. Wisely, any books that come from the new-style publishing operation are produced in collaboration with other, strongly based, publishing houses.

If publishing did not prove to be a growth area for CPAS, evangelism did. The new department offered consultancy where people with appropriate experience and good listening skills would travel to parishes, meet the clergy and lay leaders and reflect on ways that might lead to growth and faith-sharing. I did a considerable amount of this myself. I found that, in many cases, the clergy I visited were suffering from acute loneliness and often a sense of failure. Whether my suggestions were of use or not, it became clear that simply being there as a comrade-in-arms was a blessing in many cases.

I remember one visit to a vicarage where the vicar's wife broke down and wept within seconds of my arrival. She felt that her husband was getting a raw deal from some powerful figures in the parish. The going was tough and she could see his morale sapping. He arrived a few minutes later, and as we talked I discovered that he and his wife rarely took a day off and never got out for a meal or anything like a visit to the cinema. All the way home that evening, I felt desperately anxious for the two of them. I shared my thoughts with Mary and we agreed a plan of action. I knew he had no engagements the following evening, so I phoned the two of them and said that Mary and I were coming, loaded to the gills with the efforts of their nearest Chinese takeaway. We had a good time.

I sometimes think that those consultations were a good preparation for the ministry I would later have as a bishop. I saw that all the bright ideas in the world are no substitute for high morale in the vicarage and on the church council.

I worked with remarkable colleagues. The Society's general secretary, David Bubbers, gave us every encouragement. He was a former Salvation Army officer and still quite a virtuoso on the trombone. He was also capable of reducing the annual staff conference to agonies of mirth with his rendering of pieces like *The Flight of the Bumblebee*. 'We trombonists,' he would say, 'prefer to be paid on a sliding scale!'

Peter Street was a great warrior for the gospel cause. He had many years' experience in several key parishes, but his first love was leading evangelistic missions. He knew far more than I did, but graciously accepted my leadership and proved a tower of strength. Garth Hewitt joined just before I arrived.

He had served one curacy, but the Society gave him the opportunity to be a full-time gospel singer – and a good one. With his long hair, jeans and leather jackets, he was somewhat different from the very conventional image of most CPAS staff members.

Later it was a pleasure to work with Ian Knox, Jim Smith and my old friend Denis Shepheard. I had met Denis when we were both students at Oak Hill. In his day he was one of the most powerful preachers of the gospel I have ever heard. He was also very funny, with his cockney wit bubbling out irrepressibly in the pulpit and the committee room. He died in a strange bed, away from home, after preaching the last of a series of mission sermons. When he was found the following morning, it was discovered that he had been writing notes to help his wife sort out matters after his death. I was asked to preach at his funeral. The family asked that I preach the gospel and call for a response. I did so gladly, using long quotations from his last ever sermon. His favourite booklet was available at the door for those who wanted to think further about the gospel he had served so faithfully.

While I saw it as my job to advise parishes, to pass on lessons learned elsewhere and to set up missions, I did occasionally lead my own missions. In particular I was involved in setting up fortnightly young people's evangelistic meetings each spring in central London. We ran the first series in 1976, using the Friends Meeting House in Euston Road. Because of the venue, and because we wanted to create an informal mood to the meetings, we simply called it 'Meeting House'. The name stuck even when we changed the venue.

At the time the usual style of young people's evangelistic gatherings was dominated by worship music. I wanted to do something that had more content to it. Our meetings had four components. We started with twenty minutes or so of singing, with a mix of styles. After that we brought on a guest speaker to do a teaching slot. I remember that our first meeting took the theme 'Do all religions say the same thing?' Our speaker was Patrick Sookhdeo. He was the son of a Hindu and a Muslim and was himself a Christian. That seemed to me to be a unique qualification for the subject! We would then have an interval where everybody mixed and moved around. The speakers were not whisked on and off platforms like celebrities. They joined the throng. The second half of the meeting comprised a mini-concert from our singer (initially Garth Hewitt), and I ended the evening with a crisp evangelistic address and an appeal.

What excited me about these meetings was that they pulled in young people from the inner-city and inner-suburban parishes. We had relatively few large parties coming in from outer suburbia. Most of them came in car loads from small churches. We grew from an initial attendance of about 300 or so to later attendance levels of between 600 and 800. Years later in Canterbury, I met a woman in training for the ministry who could point back to Meeting House as the place where, as a teenager, she had first made her response to the gospel.

The Society gave me immense freedom to consult widely and to be involved in committees and groups that were advancing the cause of evangelism. I was allowed to spend considerable time in the Nationwide Initiative in Evangelism, I was released for a couple of lengthy spells to lead Billy Graham missions, and was encouraged to stand for election to the General Synod, where I tried to make evangelism a key issue. Finally, when the Decade of Evangelism became a key agenda of the Church of England, the Society put a package together that released me to be an official advisor to the Church of England's Board of Mission. That move revealed how much distance had been travelled since the days when CPAS was seen (with some justification) as a focal structure for those who felt that they had little in common with the official organizations of the Church of England.

Today the voluntary societies are still in transition. It could be argued that the reasons for their existence no longer obtain. When they were founded, they were filling gaping holes in the provision offered by the national Church. There were no home or overseas mission agencies and little vision for such ministry. There was no national stipend policy or centralized dispersing of income. Today the Church at national and diocesan level wants to organize and fund all its necessary activities. It is true that it has no world mission agency to rival the voluntary societies, but if those societies closed down tomorrow, the General Synod would be calling for something to be put in their place. The mind-set is very different from that of the nineteenth century.

Again the whole relationship between the traditions is different. Although the ordination of women to the priesthood opened up some sharp and painful divisions, there is more trust between evangelicals and Catholics and so-called liberals. There has been a listening process over the last twenty-five years. Evangelicals are strongly represented in the House of Bishops and in other senior positions. There is no strongly felt need for an alternative evangelical headquarters within the Church.

There is also less money to go round. There are fewer in the pews and they are being asked to find considerably more to pay for their own clergy and their diocesan services. The voluntary societies do not appear to be so important to the life of the Church and that is reflected in their difficulty in finding sufficient funds. It is sensible to ask whether the time has come for some of them to say 'job done' and release their talented staff into the mainstream of Church affairs.

It is equally sensible, however, to ask whether it is the official structures that need to think of slimming down, reducing some of their operations and handing them back to the voluntary societies. The painful reality of many dioceses is that they are facing acute financial challenges.

I could see a future where the Church of England maintains much slimmer central structures which cost the parishes less. If considerable expertise and resourcing is to be found in such societies as CPAS, the Church Army and Scripture Union (an inter-denominational organization that nevertheless knows the Anglican Church well), why should every diocese pay to duplicate such expertise and resourcing? Why could the dioceses and parishes not simply buy in areas of servicing from approved independent agencies, who would take the responsibility of employing staff and maintaining their own support structures?

In the past the arguments against this would have been doctrinal. Catholic and central churchmanship parishes would not have wanted help from evangelical agencies. I think this is less the case now in the Church as it has become. In my time in the Canterbury diocese (where there are very few traditionally evangelical parishes), I was amazed to see how many churches took up the Alpha Course, which came from a charismatic evangelical source and is also widely used by Roman Catholics!

Rather than being poor relations of the Church, I can see a future where the voluntary societies are highly valued serviceproviders. Of course there would have to be changes, both to the ways of the Church and to the workings of those societies. It could happen, however, and I have a feeling that it should happen. Indeed, when it comes to the theological colleges, it happened a very long time ago.

*   *   *

In 1987 David Bubbers announced that he would be retiring the following year. At that time I had worked on the staff, in two capacities and as a senior member, for nineteen years. I needed a new challenge and the Society needed a new general secretary. It made sense to put my name forward and several of my colleagues encouraged me to make such a move. I applied.

In due course I was shortlisted. When I saw the other names on the shortlist, I began to feel that the job was going to come in my direction. It is always difficult to be objective about oneself, especially when the other candidates were good friends. Nevertheless, I felt that no one knew the workings of CPAS to the same degree as I did. Again, in terms of nation-wide acceptance, I felt that my profile as the director of two major Billy Graham missions, plus my membership of the Standing Committee of the General Synod, put me ahead of the others who were being considered. I duly arrived for the final interviews in April 1988 and I felt that everything had gone well.

That evening – I remember I was mowing the lawn at home – the telephone rang. I was told that the post was being offered to one of the other candidates. It was hard to take it in. I felt an overwhelming sense of rejection from the very people I had served for nearly twenty years. It was not simply that I was disappointed – I was totally amazed at the decision. The next three months were very hard.

Looking back after many years, I have little difficulty in seeing that the committee made the right decision. The successful candidate, John Moore, turned out to be a brilliant administrator and leader. He brought a fresh perspective to an organization that was getting somewhat tired.

It was a painful experience at the time. Four years later, however, a letter arrived from Number 10 Downing Street, offering a job that required a change in my shirt colour. It was then that I saw fully the truth of St Paul's words about all things working together for the good of those who love God.

It's the story of my life, really.

9

Converting England

Oddly enough, the door that Bishop Mervyn Stockwood opened to welcome me to lunch belonged to his next-door neighbour.

The bishop's own house was being extensively redecorated and, as his neighbour was away for an extended period, a deal had been struck. The former Bishop of Southwark had agreed to see me because I was trying to discover why a dramatic and remarkable report, produced by the Church of England in 1945, had ended up achieving very little. He had been a member of the commission that had produced the report and what he had to say to me was illuminating.

The year was probably 1990. It was at the beginning of the worldwide Anglican 'Decade of Evangelism'. I was beginning my work as an advisor to the Church of England's Board of Mission, and I thought it might be useful to study why the report called *Towards the Conversion of England* had failed to mobilize the Church for the sort of action it claimed to be necessary. The report's 'Recommendations and Findings' section began with the following words: 'The state of the Christian religion in this country urgently calls for definite action. *That definite action is no less than the conversion of England to the Christian faith . . .'* That, to put it mildly, is not the way your average Church of England report expresses itself.

The report was an instant best-seller. It was first published in June 1945 and it had run through five further printings by November. It stirred up a considerable amount of controversy, especially with those who were angered to be told that their country needed converting in the first place. It was remarkably critical of the clergy, stating that many had little idea of how to share their faith and lead others into it. It was equally challenging to the laity, suggesting (as we have seen earlier) that the frequent excuse of having little time was more related to a preference for leisure than an over-occupation with employment.

Much of the report still sounds relevant over fifty years later. It stressed the importance of an active and mobilized laity. It spoke of the value of cells and small groups. It pointed to the need for clergy to be trained for mission, and for the laity to be able to attend training 'conventions' and 'schools for evangelism'. It suggested that the Church needed to look at what could be done through advertising campaigns. It was ahead of its time in calling for 'elasticity' in the conduct of church services to assist the 'gathering-in of non-worshippers'. It called for the appointment of diocesan missioners 'to initiate and carry into effect diocesan plans for evangelism'. It made a plea for family prayers and personal Bible reading in the home. It stressed the important place of preaching, and the need for more energy to be invested in religious education, capitalizing on the 1944 Education Act. It also said that 'the economic order of society . . . must declare the glory of God . . . [The] social environment must not be such as to give the lie to the principles of the Gospel when proclaimed, or to make it unnecessarily difficult for hearers to accept the Gospel.' It also recommended that an 'Archbishops' Council for Evangelism' be set up. That, at least, did happen. The Church has always been good at setting up committees!

Over a lunch of steak-and-kidney pie and vegetables, prepared by the bishop, and not totally hot, I asked my questions and heard Stockwood's replies. I have always been moved by the thought of a group of men and women making their plans for nationwide evangelism in a post-war England, as the flying bombs droned overhead. I have always been surprised that so little came of a report that sold like the proverbial hot cakes and spoke in such challenging terms.

What Stockwood said made sense and was to prove prophetic with regard to the fortunes of the Decade of Evangelism. First he pointed out that the report was theologically out of step with the Church of its day. It appealed to me because it was saying exactly the sort of things that evangelicals like to hear. The problem was that in 1945 evangelicals were comparatively thin on the ground, and even thinner in the leadership positions of the Church.

Stockwood also talked about the commission's chairman, Christopher Chavasse, the one-legged Bishop of Rochester, whose episcopal signature 'Christopher Roffin' was reputed to lead to numerous jokes, such as 'Hush, hush, whisper who dares, Christopher Roffin is saying his prayers'! Whether such stories were true or not, Chavasse was a striking and imposing person. He also held a very simple evangelical faith. Stockwood said that Chavasse's theology dominated the report and that few on the commission found it easy to stand up to him. The introduction to the report makes clear that not every member could subscribe to every paragraph.

The outcome was a report that was alien in tone and theology to the Church of 1945. It was also, said Stockwood, alien to the mind-set of post-war England. Those who worked on the report could only draw on their memories of pre-war England. They wrote as if, when the war was over, things would largely revert to where they had been. Stockwood said, however, that the war brought about a tremendous culture shift, and that the men returning from the front were very different people from those of the 1930s. The gap between Church and outsider was to prove far greater than expected.

As the bishop and I sipped our coffee, he touched on two other matters that again made sense and were to prove prophetic. 'The report talked about evangelism,' he said, 'but what was the big presenting problem of the post-war years? Bombed-out church buildings!' Not only were these wrecked churches staring everyone in the face, but bricks and mortar are easier things to engage with than evangelism. Thus it was that the Church of England put its post-war energies into rebuilding churches, and there was relatively little energy for anything else. The final nail in the report's coffin was the new archbishop and his concerns. *Towards the Conversion of England* was conceived in the time of William Temple, a social prophet, visionary and evangelist. Indeed, it deliberately tried to embody his very spirit. Sadly he died tragically young, before the report was completed. He was succeeded by Geoffrey Fisher, a very different man. A former headmaster, he brought a tidy-minded, headmasterly view to running a well-organized and disciplined Church. It was under his leadership that the councils of the Church embarked on a laborious revision of canon law.

And that, said Mervyn Stockwood, is why nothing very much happened to the report. I believed him.

Strangely enough, while the commission was meeting in the latter months of the war to plan for evangelism, a small group of entrepreneurial evangelicals was doing the same thing. Led by a man called Tom Rees, who had been a lay reader in Chavasse's own diocese, the group was planning a large-scale evangelistic campaign in central London.

Rees had been developing a reputation as an effective evangelist. Nevertheless, when he planned to conduct a mission in London's Westminster Central Hall, he was far from being well known. The original plans were for the autumn of 1944. With the advent of the flying bombs and V2 rockets, the plans were put on hold. A year later, however, the mission took place. Rees and his team did something that had never been done before. They booked the hall for a full month, apart from Sundays. The mission was given the title 'This is Victory!' It proved to be the right mission, with the right title, at the right time. Night after night the hall was filled, increasingly with young people. Hundreds came to faith in Christ. I knew one of the converts well. He was my brother.

Working off the back of that dramatic mission, Rees began to hold a series of evangelistic rallies each spring, for several years, in the Royal Albert Hall. One by-product of Tom Rees's large-scale mission work was that it trained up a number of people who knew how to run such missions and meetings. Those people and their skills were going to prove very significant in a few years' time.

The mood among evangelicals of all denominations in the immediate post-war years was one of great readiness to find ways to evangelize. It was exactly the right mood to receive the message of *Towards the Conversion of England*. Sadly, that mood was not reflected in the Church of England as a whole, so the evangelism that took place was left to local churches and entrepreneurial groups who convened such projects as the Christian Commando Campaigns, which tried to stimulate large amounts of lay witness.

Mervyn Stockwood was right to identify a culture shift in society as a result of the war experience. Politically it showed itself in the landslide general election victory for the Labour party. That said, there were other things in place that made England in the mid-1940s fertile soil for the gospel. The biggest of these was the fact that most of the population was aware of the gospel story. The majority of Britain's children went to Sunday school until the mid-1950s. Evangelists could speak to people who had grown up in a gospel-friendly culture. Large numbers of people had found at least some of their social life in the context of a church. The churches of the 1930s did far more than hold services. They were often the hubs around which much activity took place, such as tennis, football, badminton, drama, choirs, residential holidays and more. It was common to number the children attached to a church in terms of hundreds. Whatever else was the outcome of the amazing numerical success of the old Sunday school, it ensured that British folk religion was well informed and dominantly Christian.

Dick Williams, in his biography of Archbishop Stuart Blanch, points out that in the 1930s Blanch was actively involved in a south London church all through his teenage years, and yet for all that time he sat outside any Christian commitment. That was not uncommon in those days. Churches carried large fringes, and the effect of this was that the England of the 1940s was full of people in which the seeds of the gospel had been sown. It was tailor-made for the winsome preaching evangelist. The Church of England, by sidelining its report on evangelism, probably lost the greatest opportunity it has had in modern history to draw thousands into its congregations. As it was, the independents managed to harvest something, and this story of official structures failing and the independents having to move in is one that will be repeated.

In the autumn of 1946 a lanky, courteous American from North Carolina began a series of 360 meetings throughout Britain and Europe. In later life he was often heard to say that the British taught him a great deal about evangelism during those days. His name was Billy Graham, and the extended visit was largely unnoticed at the time. In the years that were to follow, he developed into the biggest name in evangelism in the United States since the idiosyncratic Billy Sunday. In 1949 he led a tent mission in Los Angeles that suddenly broke into the national headlines of the United States. Over the next few years, he and his team drew massive attendance figures for their 'crusades' in major American cities.

In 1952 Graham was invited by the Evangelical Alliance to address a gathering of English ministers in Church House, Westminster. He spoke at length about what was happening in the American crusades. He talked frankly about the potential for emotionalism in large gatherings, he admitted the dangers of popular evangelists being corrupted by money, and he talked openly about the problem of converts who 'did not last'. When he was finished, he had to answer questions for a further hour. He made a profound impression.

The text of his address was published and widely circulated. It was inevitable that an invitation to England would follow, and it did. Before he returned to America Graham accepted an invitation from Tom Rees to speak at one of Rees's Albert Hall rallies. Rees virtually offered his team to help with anything that Graham might do. It was a generous and unselfish offer, and it helped greatly when in 1954 the Greater London Crusade opened its doors at the Harringay Arena on a snowy 1st March.

What followed can hardly be exaggerated. It must have been the most monumental evangelistic campaign in Britain since the days of D. L. Moody, and possibly since the times of Wesley and Whitefield. For twelve long weeks the crowds came to Harringay. On several occasions, last-minute decisions were made to hold two briefer, successive meetings in the 11,400-seater hall, and on at least one occasion, when I was there, three meetings were held. Extra meetings were held in Trafalgar Square, and in Hyde Park on Good Friday when 40,000 people gathered to hear Graham preach on the cross. Above the preacher – and many commented on this – two vapour trails formed a cross in the sky. Whether it was a fortuitous accident, or whether a couple of pilots had an appropriate agenda, we shall never know.

Early in the crusade it was discovered that Post Office land lines could be used to carry the meetings to other locations. Very quickly scores of ancillary missions to the main crusade were set up using sound relays, drawing in thousands more each night.

The originally sceptical and hostile press totally changed its tune. The Harringay meetings and Graham himself began to get friendly and extensive coverage. And still the crowds came every night. One feature of London evening life during the period was the sound of hymn-singing on public transport. It was both comical and moving to stand on an underground platform as the tube trains came in. As soon as the automatic doors slid open, out would come the sound of community hymn-singing. The doors would close, the train moved on, another arrived, the doors opened, and yet more singing filled the station.

After twelve exhausting weeks of meetings in Harringay, plus numerous other day-time commitments, the crusade came to a close in Wembley Stadium. At least that was the plan. It became clear to the organizers that even Wembley would prove too small. The White City Stadium was booked for an extra meeting in the afternoon. That siphoned off 67,000 people and required a sound overflow in the nearby Queen's Park Rangers football ground. In the evening a further 120,000 people gathered for the last meeting of the Greater London Crusade, and among those who took part was the Archbishop of Canterbury.

I was a student at Queen Mary College in east London during that time, and helped as one of the many stewards at Harringay. I was in rehearsals with the college drama group for a production that spring, and I remember tentatively suggesting that other members of the cast and production team might like to come and hear Billy Graham. With very little difficulty, we filled a bus and went in style. That sort of thing was happening at churches, schools, colleges, offices, factories and clubs.

I have little doubt that the effects of that crusade were deep and far-reaching. There were certainly many genuine converts. In the Church of England the evangelical minority felt affirmed and gained greater self-confidence in advancing their cause. Many in the other traditions were impressed not only with Billy Graham himself, but also with the need to evangelize, and with the apparent power of simple Bible exposition – even in a scientific age. Perhaps the most significant development was a wave of young people offering for Christian ministry as a result of being involved as counsellors in the crusade. That role required hundreds to be ready every night to talk with those who came forward. It was often, for many, the first real experience of leading others to faith in Christ. The ordinands who came out of the Harringay phenomenon brought with them a recognition that evangelism was the top priority in Christian ministry. It was to prove a foundation for the evangelical renaissance that began to be visible in the 1960s and has been a fact of Church life ever since.

Thirty years after Harringay, I stood on the platform in Bristol City's football ground to address a crowd of 31,000 people and to welcome Billy Graham back to Britain to begin the great Mission England project. This time I was the national director of the mission. It was to be one of the greatest moments of my life, but I have to admit that for all the apparent success of Mission England, it made nowhere near the impact of the astonishing crusade of 1954. It is worth asking why . . .

I think the main reason for the difference is that in 1954 we were still preaching to those who were the products of an openly Christian culture, who knew the alphabet of faith even if they had not got as far as the joined-up writing of commitment. Again, the Sunday school background of many of Graham's hearers in 1954 was something that was no longer true of the under-thirties in that crowd at Bristol. It was not until the later 1950s that the Sunday school lost its hold, and nothing was left in its place.

Much has been written about the effects of the 1960s. It became the decade when long-established traditions were challenged and even ridiculed. No longer did the media accord a touch of deference to Church leaders. A mood of rebelliousness was to be found in much of the popular music of the day. The motor car and the leisure industry were creating exciting alternatives to the local church's children's activities on Sunday afternoons in often dingy church halls. Billy

Graham came in 1961 for a crusade in Manchester (where he was ill and unable to preach at some of the meetings), and again in 1966 and 1967 to London for crusades that were well planned, well attended and apparently successful. There was, however, nothing like the public stirring that came at Harringay.

By this time many Church leaders, including evangelicals, were beginning to look critically at crusade evangelism. It was not that they were denying the value of what happened in the mid-1950s, but they recognized the social and cultural changes that had taken place since those days. Much more emphasis began to be placed on the primacy of the local church in evangelism. With the sad shrinkage of unattended children coming to the old-style Sunday school, many churches across the denominations began to put the emphasis on reaching the whole family. Family Services were a growth area. In the mid-1960s I was leading a small church in Essex, and the only real area of growth was our weekly Family Service.

With the new emphasis on the local church there came, perhaps, an unrecognized scepticism of the value of anything big. Dramatic visions of converting England did not readily come to mind in any of the mainstream denominations. The Church of England was wrestling with plans to reunite with Methodism. It was also beginning to face the prospect that, for all the increased numbers of men coming forward for the priesthood, retirements, deaths and a tailing-off of recruits towards the end of the decade meant that new thinking about ministry could not be avoided.

One of the big distractions of the era was 'South Bank religion' and the challenge of the radicals usually associated with Stockwood's Diocese of Southwark. It was in 1963 that John

Robinson (one of Stockwood's suffragan bishops) published *Honest to God*. Robinson's small book challenged the traditional images of God. The tabloid coverage of his book gave the impression that we had an unbelieving bishop in our midst. Archbishop Michael Ramsey was deeply concerned and went so far as to write and publish a rebuttal, which was an extraordinary step to take.

In spite of the fact that evangelism was not getting top billing during this period, the Evangelical Alliance, at its assembly in 1966, called for:

> . . . the setting up of a Commission on Evangelism, which will prayerfully consider and recommend the best means of reaching the unchurched masses at national, local and personal levels, bearing in mind the need to co-ordinate existing endeavours where possible and *specifically to promote a new emphasis on personal evangelism*. (my italics)

I was on the reference group of the commission and wrote the section of the final report on the place of literature in evangelism. That report, entitled *On the Other Side*, was published two years later. It proved to be a very low-key and realistic assessment of the situation. It recognized that it would probably prove a disappointment to many of its readers hoping to find some master plan for the conversion of England. It was critical of crusade evangelism, without discounting it entirely.

> The time has gone for 'vicarious' evangelism in which Christians seek to transfer their own responsibility either to professionals or even to the impersonal method . . . Personal evangelism is still the prime method, and the hope of this Commission is that this will be stimulated by the reading of the report. (p. 179)

Much good stuff can be found in that report, but whether many looked for it I am not so sure.

The mind-set of the 1960s carried over into the 70s. By this time the agenda of the charismatic movement was dominating the very church groupings that usually demonstrated a concern for widespread evangelism. Whether congregations and their leaders were throwing themselves into renewal issues and conferences, or whether they were mounting an opposition to such matters, the renewal agenda dominated the concerns of evangelical churches for the opening years of the decade. The glorious exception to this preoccupation came from charismatic leader David Watson. While discussions about the nature and need of evangelism were to go round in circles throughout the decade, Watson led an evangelizing church in York and numerous effective missions throughout the country. He proved to be the independent who got on with things during this period.

There were, however, still some attempts to make evangelism happen across the churches, and two of them involved the leadership of the Church of England and the other major denominations. The evangelicals, for their part, called a conference in 1972 in a Morecambe holiday camp. The 'Strategy for Evangelism' conference, sponsored by the Evangelical Alliance and the Church of England Evangelical Council, struggled through several days of bitterly cold weather – it was supposed to be spring – and produced very little either by way of grand challenges to the Church or resourcing for its members. The mood of the conference was very much in line with *On the Other Side*. It did at least keep the agenda alive, and the title revealed that evangelism was something that deserved a strategy.

Many of those who came to the conference from northern

churches, however, had another agenda on their minds. The Archbishop of York, Donald Coggan, had begun to discuss with senior leaders of all denominations the possibility of finding ways to bring about a united emphasis on evangelism throughout the churches in northern England. After several years of discussion and planning, the church leaders issued their 'Call to the North' in Holy Week 1973. There was to be no great concerted mission. Rather, beginning from the leaders themselves, there was to be a companionship across the denominations in evangelism. Perhaps the biggest manifestation of this companionship was a massive house-to-house distribution of Mark's Gospel throughout northern England, involving people from 9,000 churches.

It was about this time that some individuals began to suggest a further invitation to Billy Graham. The natural allies of Graham, however, were caught up in the more sceptical moods of *On the Other Side* and the Strategy for Evangelism conference. Discussions at the Evangelical Alliance led to yet another working group to see if there was any way ahead that would capture the imagination of the churches. Chaired officially by John Stott, but actually by Tom Houston of the Bible Society, the group came up with an idea that it wanted to commend to all the churches and traditions, and not merely to the evangelicals.

This new report was called *Let My People Grow!* It reflected the growing interest, not least on the part of Houston himself, in the American Church Growth school of thought. Rather than putting the focus on gathering people and preaching to them, Church Growth thinking began by identifying growing churches and analysing what they were doing that might explain their evangelistic success.

The report was hawked around the denominations, but met

with little enthusiasm. Many were put off by its talk of setting goals for numerical growth. What the report did achieve, however, was continuing discussion and concern for finding a way or ways to stimulate widespread evangelism. *Let My People Grow!* got thumbs down all round, but those who voted it down recognized that they had to find something better. There was also a feeling that bringing Graham back was not the answer and that evangelism had to be something that all the traditions in the Churches owned.

In 1974 Donald Coggan became the Archbishop of Canterbury. He came to the office fresh from the encouragements of the Call to the North. He came wanting to do something similar for the whole nation. With Stuart Blanch, Bishop of Liverpool, moving to become the Archbishop of York, the country now had two archbishops who thought in similar terms and who had already worked together in a large-scale call to evangelism. Something was inevitably going to happen, and people did not have to wait for very long.

Coggan, probably with too little consultation and with no supportive infrastructure in place, led a 'Call to the Nation' on behalf of Blanch and himself. He hoped that he could use his office to stimulate a time of national soul-searching. He also hoped that this would open up opportunities for church members to engage in a multitude of marketplace discussions about their faith. Two terse and challenging questions were put to the British people: 'What sort of society do we want?' and 'What sort of people do we need to be in order to achieve it?'

The Call was launched in October 1976. The nation was told through the media five days before the congregations were officially called into the action the following Sunday. Looking back, it is hard to avoid the feeling that the initiative was something of a flop. Archbishop Coggan received 27,000 letters of support from the great British public, but I know from personal experience that what many people 'heard' Coggan say was not what he was trying to say. One aristocratic lady who worshipped in our church in Surrey wrote to the vicar and said that the Call had made her realize that she should no longer support a church so trendy as to experiment with alternatives to the Prayer Book.

To his credit, however, Coggan believed that if you never try to do things then you will never see things done. Within a year or so of the Call to the Nation, he became aware of the discussions taking place over *Let My People Grow!* and also of the repeated mutterings of some that there was still a job for Billy Graham to do. By this time, I had joined the mutterers.

Key Church leaders concerned about evangelism were called for discussions in Lambeth Palace. Out of these discussions another initiative was born. It was initially to be known as the 'National Initiative in Evangelism'. Very soon the name was modified. Some critics were anxious about the use of the word 'national' in the title. They feared that this appeared to suggest a top-down, blanket strategy. Echoing the thinking of *On the Other Side* and the Call to the North, they suggested that 'nationwide' was a more helpful term. The way forward, they suggested, should be one of stimulating evangelism in many ways from individual congregations and from churches working in local groupings.

The Nationwide Initiative in Evangelism (NIE) was organized by a central committee to which people were nominated by various sponsoring bodies. I found myself in the ridiculous position of being nominated to the committee by the Evangelical Alliance, who were at the same time distancing themselves politically from the self-same committee. The

Alliance was, to be fair, walking a tightrope in this sort of exercise, since a strong section of their membership disapproved of any co-operation with groups that did not share their theological position. The Alliance even ran a parallel project to NIE which they called, prophetically perhaps, the 'Decade of Evangelism'.

Much was made at the time of a 'convergence' in theological thinking about evangelism between the evangelical pronouncements of the Lausanne Conference of 1974, and the latest statements on evangelization to come from the Roman Catholics and the World Council of Churches.

Attempts were made by the central committee to set up regional NIE committees, only to find that the different denominations had their own regional boundaries and such matters were far more difficult to rationalize than one might suppose. The crucial point towards which the NIE central group was planning, led by the brilliant Methodist Donald English, was a conference at Nottingham University in the late summer of 1980.

On the first night of this conference the Archbishop of Canterbury was due to speak. When the day came, however, it was a new archbishop – Robert Runcie. The Archbishop came to the platform jeered and heckled by Paisleyite demonstraters who had slipped into the hall unnoticed. The congregation spontaneously rose to sing a hymn of praise to drown the protesters, who were, shall we say, encouraged to leave and did so. The atmosphere was electric and there was immense warmth towards Runcie in the light of the circumstances.

He began to speak. I have always liked Runcie, but many of us who heard him that night realized that NIE was not to be his vision. As we packed up after a conference which had been intended to launch a project, many of us knew in our hearts that we were actually staring at its imminent end. Somewhere around a year later, NIE was dead and the dear man hired to be its executive secretary was seeking another job. It was a case of *Towards the Conversion of England* all over again. The archbishop who inspired it was not the archbishop into whose lap it was dropped.

By this time I – and I was not alone – decided that the time had come to back away from the official structures and go independent. On a hot July day in 1981 a small group of us boarded a plane at Heathrow and flew to Nice. The plan was to interrupt somebody's holiday and talk about a new sort of mission to the people of England. Waiting for us at the other end of our journey was Billy Graham.

We met in the basement of a hotel near the seaside airport. With me was Clive Calver, the dynamic leader of British Youth for Christ, Maurice Rowlandson, the director of Graham's office in London, and David Rennie, a business-man and long-term associate of Billy Graham's work in Europe and the United Kingdom. There was one other member of our party, Eddie Gibbs. Eddie worked on church growth consultancy with the Bible Society. He and I had been kindred spirits since we trained together for the ministry at Oak Hill. For some time Eddie and I had daydreamed together over lunch meetings about the possibility of tying in church growth programmes with Billy Graham's sort of ministry. Our thinking was almost identical, and now we put our plan to Dr Graham. We wanted him to come and lead crusade-type missions in several English regional cities. We wanted him to come after a prolonged period of congregational preparation, which would be designed to make churches face up to their need to be more welcoming and more able to grow. We also wanted Billy Graham's ministry

to be the incentive for local church mission and the stimula-
tor of more after he had gone.

The plans would make big demands of the American evangelist, who was now in his sixties. We would need two to three
months of his time in the summer of 1984. To our surprise
Graham warmed almost immediately to what he heard. 'If
you were asking me to come and do evangelism for you, I
don't think I would be interested,' he said. 'But if you are
asking me to come and do evangelism *with* you, that's a different matter!'

It was at that point we had to tell Graham that we had no
backing for our initiative. We said there was a great deal of
scepticism in England as to whether Billy Graham would
agree to another mission. We said there was also some doubt
about the value of the old-style crusade simply by itself. We
told him that if we went back and spoke to English Church
leaders, laid out the plan, and said that he was willing to come
if he was invited to operate along the lines of the plan, then
we believed we could come back to him with a credible invitation. I sensed that one of Billy's aides, Walter Smyth, was a
little unconvinced! Billy, however, was in a good mood. He
encouraged us to see if we could get that invitation, and he
even started talking about the practical problems of outdoor
meetings and the British weather. I was convinced that he
wanted to come.

By the spring of 1982, after months of meetings and consultations, we had a solid invitation from areas that focused
on Birmingham, Liverpool/Manchester, Norwich/Ipswich,
Bristol and Sunderland. We put the invitation formally to Dr
Graham when he was in this country for a brief trip, and he
agreed to come.

From the summer of 1982 to the starting date of the 12th

May 1984, it seemed that my life was lived more in a car than anywhere else. I had been asked to be the national director for the project, and my suggested title of Mission England was accepted. Eddie Gibbs headed up a remarkable training pro-gramme which involved many of the 6,000 churches that came on board.

It was not long before churches in Sheffield were pressing to have their city included as an extra venue. This simply could not be done for 1984, but after a great deal of negotiation, Graham agreed to return in 1985 to take a week of meetings in Sheffield. That later phase was to prove significant in that we discovered we could mount fifty smaller extra missions from Sheffield by using direct-link satellite. This greatly added to the outreach and impact, and it was something which we further developed in 1989 when Graham returned for a three-venue mission to Greater London.

The great value of using Dr Graham in provincial cities, as opposed to metropolitan London, was that the sheer scale of his operation made Jesus Christ a major topic of public con-versation. Our cities were chosen with care. We went for places with good daily regional newspapers and good local radio and television services. It had always been my argument for using Billy Graham that, quite apart from anything that happened in the meetings, the sheer newsworthiness of those meetings ensured that Christians had ideal conditions to talk about their faith in everyday situations.

We felt that the plan would not work so well in London. It so happened that a strong group of churches in the London area invited Luis Palau to come for a mission, first to speak in local missions all round the Greater London area in 1983 (which I thought was a brilliant idea), and in 1984 to come to a central London football stadium and conduct a long crusade-type mission. I felt that the central London mission was over-ambitious, and the attendances were, in the main, disappointing. Nevertheless, Palau's ministry was effective for those who came – and over the weeks a large number of people attended.

The effect of the two missions was that while the official, top-down NIE hardly progressed beyond talk and planning and then faded from view, independents yet again made some large-scale evangelism happen in England. Again the parallels to the 1940s and the work of Tom Rees, when *Towards the Conversion of England* was foundering, are obvious. Of course it has to be acknowledged that the independent initiatives usually reflect only one tradition within the Churches, namely Evangelicalism. Over the years I frequently heard the criticism that evangelicals always end up dominating any attempt that the wider Church makes to initiate evangelism. It is very difficult to know how to deal with such a criticism. To the evangelical, evangelism is the top priority. It is not reasonable to suggest that we should stop, or that we should wait until everybody can agree to a course of evangelistic action.

I am reminded of a story about the nineteenth-century American evangelist D. L. Moody. Someone once said to him, 'Sir, I do not care for your method of evangelism.'

'Pray tell me, what method do you use?' asked Moody.

Haughtily the other man replied, 'I use no method of evangelism.'

'Then, sir,' replied Moody, 'I would rather use the method I use than the method you don't use!'

Graham returned in 1989 to conduct a three-venue mission to Greater London. Once again I was asked to be the overall director, but on this occasion I was reluctant to do so. It was around the time that my organization, CPAS, was facing a change of leadership and I knew I had to consider the direction of my future ministry. I wrote to the Archbishop of Canterbury for advice. Very few people knew that when I went to the United States in 1988 on behalf of a group of London church leaders with an invitation to lead a mission the following year, I was also carrying a handwritten note from Archbishop Runcie. I watched Billy Graham open the letter and read it. I do not know what it said, but it made the American evangelist say 'yes' to London on the spot. I have always had a feeling that Graham might not have come if it had not been for Runcie's letter.

The Archbishop encouraged me to set my plans aside and lead the mission. We packed West Ham football ground, broke the attendance record at Crystal Palace athletics stadium (in spite of widespread transport strikes) and filled Earl's Court for a week, with 250 'Livelink' satellite television venues joining in around the British Isles.

Once again, I felt that we had been involved in a very successful mission. I was equally sure, however, that we had not tapped into the soul of the nation in the way that Graham's 1954 crusade had done. The world was now a different place.

The 1989 mission – we called it simply Mission 89 – ended with a large gathering in Wembley Stadium. Some 80,000 people braved torrential rain to hear Graham preach in England probably for the last time. For me that meeting came in the middle of a frenetic few days. The General Synod was meeting in York and I had to be there for the Friday and back for the Sunday. I flew to Heathrow on the Saturday and back to York for the Sunday. I had to be back on the Sunday because I wanted to speak in a key debate that afternoon. The debate was about whether the Church of England should respond to the call of the 1988 Lambeth Conference and declare the final decade of the twentieth century a 'Decade of Evangelism'. As I said my goodbyes to Billy at Wembley, he said quietly, 'I'll be praying for that debate tomorrow.' The debate went well and the General Synod, almost with enthusiasm though not quite, voted to go ahead.

Much nonsense appeared in the press about the Decade of Evangelism. It was never intended to be a national campaign. It was never intended to be a specific targeting of Jews, Muslims and those of other faith communities as some alleged. Nor was the Decade a bright idea that George Carey brought with him when he became Archbishop in 1991. The idea came from African bishops in 1988 and the General Synod voted for it when Runcie was still in office.

We were now into the 1990s and into another official exercise in nationwide evangelism. In spite of its Anglican origins, the other denominations joined in and the Roman Catholics claimed that they had been thinking of a 'Decade of Evangelization' before the rest of us in any case! The newly restructured Board of Mission in Church House took responsibility for getting the Decade launched centrally. It was, however, given no extra funds in 1990 or, indeed, at any time during the subsequent ten years. We were able to appoint an officer for the Decade, but that was entirely because the new archbishop (a superb fund-raiser) provided money for this to happen.

In the early months of discussion about the way forward, I found myself in the middle of a friendly but very real conflict of opinions. I wanted to see a strong lead from the centre. One or two other key people were anxious that this would be seen as another top-down exercise which the parishes would not welcome. There was also some anxiety about my own involvement, coming as I did straight from a high-profile Billy Graham mission. Once again we were into this dilemma of evangelicals being criticized for being the group in the Church most ready to get involved in evangelism.

To be quite frank, a whole lot of politics was going on. Eventually Nigel McCullough, then Bishop of Taunton, was placed firmly in the chair of a new Decade of Evangelism Committee. It was the right choice, but the delay in getting to it and the further delay in finding John Finney as our Decade officer both served to slow the early momentum. This was to prove costly in the light of what was to happen in November 1992.

The main aim of the Decade was to achieve a change in attitude and priorities in a basically pastoral Church. The exercise was not about setting goals for churches and dioceses so much as learning how to be a different sort of Church – one that could effectively live out and share the gospel in the sort of society that now exists. The whole thing was about concentration and focus.

In November 1992 the issue of ordaining women as priests came to the General Synod. There was a tense build-up to the debate, and a tense but fine debate. The required two-thirds majority was narrowly gained and the Church of England decided to ordain women to the priesthood. The decision was a painful one for very many. Just under a third of the Church of England disagreed with the decision, and there were calls from within those ranks to leave for Roman Catholicism or Orthodoxy. About a quarter of the evangelical constituency saw the vote as evidence of a firmly rooted liberalism in the Church at large. Feelings were high. The Archbishops of Canterbury and York moved quickly to find a way to keep those who were disappointed within the Church of England. After several tense months, an Act of Synod was passed that established, among other things, 'provincial episcopal visi-

tors'. These were new bishops, officially suffragans to the archbishops, who were meant to give reassuring support to that
section of the Church which could not recognize women
priests or accept the ministry of those bishops who could.

Whatever else can be said about these developments, it has
to be recognized that they did not help the cause of the
Decade of Evangelism. The truth was that the biggest issue
facing the Church was not to do with its mission but to do
with its divided ministry. The Act of Synod, however, showed
some signs of being welcomed and easing pain.

It was then that something else happened. News began to
break that the Church Commissioners had made serious mistakes in their investment policies and that the Church had lost
some £800 million. The shock waves of this were soon felt. It
was a case of pain on top of pain. Clergy morale plummeted.
One priest wrote to ask me when and how clergy redundan-
cies would be announced. Once again, it has to be said that
these sorts of issues do not go easily with an attempt to get the
whole Church focused on mission and learning how to
evangelize.

A new Synod was voted into office in 1995. When its
members began to pick up and read their papers, it became
clear that the five years that were to follow would be dominated by one main issue. We were called to engage in a wholesale revision of the Church's liturgy. There were to be new
services and a new book, and everything would have to be
debated through the House of Bishops and the General
Synod, and tested in the parishes.

Looking back, I feel that the decision to concentrate on
revising our liturgy was the final blow to the vision of a
Decade of Evangelism. It may have been motivated by
mission concerns, but it had the effect of taking the focus off

the mission that was supposed to be in hand. Church historians of a later age may well describe the 1990s as a Decade of Theological Controversy, a Decade of Financial Anxiety and a Decade of Liturgical Revision. I very much doubt whether it will be seen as ten years when evangelism became the heartbeat of the national Church. This is not to deny, however, that some very good things happened.

On the theological front there were giant strides forward in defining evangelism itself. After thirty years in the wilderness, it was possible to say again that evangelism actually had something to do with the story of Jesus Christ, his life, death and resurrection! On the strategic front it became widely recognized that most people came to faith not as a sudden crisis on hearing words, but as a process of discoveries based on relationships. All traditions began to find common ground in this recognition that people usually came to faith after they discovered and became comfortable in the community of faith – belonging came before believing. We began to talk about *process conversion* rather than *crisis conversion*.

A number of dioceses appointed diocesan missioners or advisors in evangelism – an idea that could be traced back to *Towards the Conversion of England*. As the Decade came to an end, the Churches of all denominations worked together successfully to press the government to recognize that the millennium was in fact a Christian festival and that this required official recognition in the planned national celebrations.

That said, however, the Decade of Evangelism was a case of history repeating itself. The Church will always find that other things get in the way of an intention to concentrate on evangelism, whether it be rebuilding bombed churches or engaging in liturgical revision. Theology is always a basic problem when you try to move from talk about evangelism to the actual doing of it. The fact of the matter is that the Church of England does not have a consensus when it comes to understanding what the gospel is and why the Church exists. It has always worked on the principle that if it keeps itself busy trying to 'be there' for people and maintaining public worship, it will not get caught out on this question!

History also repeated itself in other ways. While relatively little was happening because of the official activity, independents took centre stage. The Decade of Evangelism was the Decade of Alpha. Alpha was the invention of a charismatic evangelical parish in London. Holy Trinity, Brompton, began to market skilfully the course it had developed for its own use. It was designed to introduce seekers to the content and spirit of the Christian faith. It embodied the principle of process evangelism and 'belonging before believing'. The take-up around the country (and beyond) was astonishing. Thousands of churches, from independent chapels to the Roman Catholic cathedral in Westminster, became 'Alpha churches'. Other similar courses, reflecting different emphases but setting out to do the same job, were also published. Very many people found these courses life-changing.

In the Church of England the two archbishops launched their own independent initiative called Springboard. Springboard started as a small agency utilizing the gifts of Bishop Michael Marshall and Canon Michael Green, an Anglo-Catholic and an evangelical. It developed a valuable ministry of courses and training for laypeople and clergy in diocese after diocese. Once again we had caught up the suggestions of *Towards the Conversion of England*.

At a very different level, the evangelist Dan Cozens began to conduct his 'Walks of a Thousand Men'. He recruited large numbers of men to live rough and to walk through regions of the country where preparations had been made in advance for meetings, pub visits, door-to-door visitations and house meetings. His great dream in all this was to 'go outside the camp' with the gospel and to get men – the silent minority in our congregations – to pluck up their courage and share their faith.

While it could be argued that these things would have happened in any case, I think it is fair to say that the official call for a Decade of Evangelism created a fair wind for them and greatly assisted in their flourishing. I do not believe the Decade was a flop. It achieved immeasurably more than NIE, but the one thing it set out to do was the one thing that circumstances made impossible. It could not change the Church into a body of people who wanted to convert England to the Christian faith. The vision of that small group of men and women who planned away in the closing years of the Second World War has yet to be realized.

Perhaps the truth that we have to face is that we are not dealing here with things that can be planned or motivated from the central structures. We are dealing with what is the property of the Holy Spirit, and he has a strange habit of making things happen which nobody expects, let alone writes reports about. If the Church of England in the eighteenth century had officially tried to launch a spiritual awakening, I think we would still be waiting for it to happen.

Thank God for George Whitefield and the Wesley brothers!

10

'Too Much Sin and Too Much Nod!'

'On a point of order, Madam Chairman,' cried Tom Butler, Bishop of Southwark, 'under Standing Order 36(d)(iv) I call for a division by Houses on this amendment.'

The chairman, Archdeacon Judith Rose, the highest-ranking woman priest in the Church of England, with a lawyer at her side, came back with the correct response: 'Are there twenty-five people standing to support you?'

What followed brought a gasp from the General Synod, followed by laughter and applause. Every single bishop in the Synod leapt to his feet.

General Synod meetings at York University are held every summer immediately after the ending of the university term. They have a totally different character from the meetings held in November in the famous circular debating chamber of Church House. Dress is casual. It needs to be, as the temperature and atmosphere in the meeting hall can often be stifling. During debates members slip down to the artificial lake which surrounds the hall, and sit on the concrete steps sipping coffee and sharing thoughts. In the late evening the summer air is full of laughter as members sit and chat outside the various bars of the halls of residence.

On the Sunday buses take all, except those who insist on walking, into York for the service in the minster. For me that service was one of the highlights of the year. The minster knows how to present a dignified service with a touch of the informal. There would always be a chuckle or two as the congregation would be taught some new chant before the service began. The preacher would normally be one of the archbishops. At my last such service I found it very hard to control the lump in my throat and difficult to see through misted eyes.

Fringe meetings and informal interviews were constantly taking place. Bishops would slip out to have quick discussions with future colleagues, and if you wanted to play the private detective you could anticipate several future appointments long before any announcement in the press.

For all the obvious enjoyment and friendship, however, debates could sometimes be tense, and the debate in which the bishops leapt to their feet was just such a case. For reasons that will become obvious, I want to take some time to spell out the story surrounding this particular debate.

The year was 1997 and the motion was about sexuality, which usually means that it is actually about homosexuality. All through my time in General Synod, which began in 1985 and ended in York in the summer of 2000, homosexuality was the lurking issue that would not go away. Ten years earlier, the Reverend Tony Higton of Chelmsford diocese had decided to bring the matter fully into the open. He put down a private member's motion which, in very uncompromising terms, called for Synod to condemn homosexual practices as 'sinful in all circumstances' and for 'Christian leaders to be exemplary in all spheres of morality, including

sexual morality, as a condition of being appointed to and
remaining in office'.

The motion very quickly got a massive list of supporting
signatures and a debate was scheduled for the November sessions of that year. It was widely believed by General Synod
members that some bishops had knowingly ordained a
number of clergy who were practising homosexuals, and the
press had a great time plastering the issue over their pages in
the days leading up to the debate.

The 1987 House of Bishops was clearly very uncomfortable
at the prospect of this debate. This was before my time as a
member of that House, but I can well imagine the angst that
would have been felt, and for good reasons. This was, and
remains, a major issue. To be bounced into an ill-prepared and
possibly ill-tempered debate was hardly likely to promote
clear and sensitive thinking. Then I could well imagine
another reason for the bishops' discomfort. The gay question
is not simply an issue suited to debating chambers. It is about
people – people who find themselves to be the way they are
and who have deep feelings and, in some cases, strong bonds
of affection. Many Christians who take a strong conservative
line on homosexual practices, as I do, still feel it is wrong to
throw long-range resolutions at people who ought to be
engaged in a caring and personal way. I probably did not hold
that view in 1987, but I have come to such a view over the years
since.

In the event the most clear-cut evangelical bishop in the
General Synod, Michael Baughen, put forward a more
gently worded amendment 'as an endeavour to balance a
more accurate biblical content with a greater gentleness of
expression'. His amendment had the effect of a replacement
motion, saying most of the things that Higton wanted to say,

but stressing sexual morality as a response to God's love, with adultery, fornication and homosexual genital acts as departures from an ideal. Although Michael Baughen spoke only as an individual member, few present doubted that this amendment was the de facto official offering from the bishops. After a long debate in front of an overcrowded public gallery, the Baughen amendment, slightly strengthened in one place, was overwhelmingly passed by 403 votes to 8 with 13 abstentions.

The House of Bishops, however, remained unhappy with what had taken place in the 1987 General Synod debate. Some of them disliked the motion for which they had voted and most were dismayed at what they considered to be the unhelpful atmosphere created by the debate itself. It was felt that a more reflective position needed to be put before the Church at large – one that had not come to birth in the polarized circumstances of a debating chamber. In December 1991 the House published a report entitled *Issues in Human Sexuality*.

The report called itself a 'Statement by the House of Bishops' and declared its purpose to be that of promoting 'an educational process as a result of which Christians may become more informed about and understanding of certain human realities'. The preface also contained a phrase that would return to haunt the bishops in years to come: 'This Statement – which we do not pretend to be the last word on the subject . . .' The hope of the House was that the statement would receive widespread study by clergy chapters and congregations.

It seemed to me at the time that the bishops had not made up their minds as to whether the statement was a discussion document or an official position. It was never brought to the floor of the General Synod for debate, and therefore it never received a commendation from that body. It modestly said that it was not the last word on the subject, but it quickly became clear that the bishops were acting on it quite strictly when it came to the vexing question of whether or not to ordain practising homosexual people.

At the heart of the statement was an apparent double standard. It seemed to require celibacy and chastity from unmarried clergy, and thus gay priests could not engage in sexual activity and remain in orders. On the other hand, it said that the laity had to be allowed to follow their consciences on these matters. This distinction tended to make enemies both from those who advocated a more tolerant attitude regarding gay sex, and those who wanted to see a firm 'no' all round in these matters.

I would contend that the statement got it right. It said that homosexual love could not be regarded as on a par with marriage and that, for Christ, 'it is not unreasonable to infer that he regarded heterosexual love as the God-given pattern'. It called priests to live out the teaching of the Church, because they were meant to exemplify what was believed to be God's will. On the other hand, it recognized that laypeople in our congregations are at different stages in their discipleship and that blanket disciplines could obscure the grace of God from those who are seeking or finding their way towards faith.

Six years after the publication of the statement, there was little evidence that it had received the sort of widespread study the bishops had wanted. It was also true to say that the issues were still bubbling away and that this was being helped by skilful lobbying from the Lesbian and Gay Christian Movement. Out of the blue, in late 1996, the Archdeacon of Southwark put down a private member's motion which was phrased as follows:

That this Synod

(a) commend for discussion in the dioceses the House of Bishops' report *Issues in Human Sexuality* and acknowledge that it is not the last word on the subject;

(b) in particular, urge deanery synods, clergy chapters and congregations to find time for prayerful study and reflection on the issues addressed by the report.

By the spring of 1997 it was clear that the motion had attracted enough support to make a debate unavoidable. History was repeating itself. Once again the bishops found themselves being wrong-footed.

It might be felt that such discomfort was irrational. After all, the Archdeacon of Southwark was only asking that the bishops' statement be taken more seriously. There were, however, two reasons why the bishops felt that there was more to this motion than met the eye. The first was the inclusion in the wording of the phrase from the statement's preface, 'it is not the last word on the subject'. As people began to anticipate the debate, those words were being picked up. Could it be that the bishops expected to say more, and could the 'more' be something very different from their first comments? It became clear that the Lesbian and Gay Christian Movement were claiming that this debate was a move in a direction that they wished to see.

The second reason why the bishops were feeling uneasy was that once a motion is tabled for debate, other members are free to put down amendments. There was the real danger that the General Synod could be pushed by amendments either to take a tougher line on the subject, or to vote for a more liberal position. Either way, there was a real danger of a polarized Synod and an ugly debate. Of one thing we could be certain: the media would be at York in force and there would be no lack of demonstrations and lobbying from the gay community.

Perhaps we (I was now a member of the House of Bishops) should have let things take their course. Had we done so, I am quite sure that we would have ended up with a motion at least as conservative as that of 1987. I have a feeling, however, that a rift within the House of Bishops might also have been exposed. It would not have been a big one, but the unease of some towards the 1987 motion might have been voiced. There might also have been a small breaking in the ranks regarding the 1991 statement itself.

All this will doubtless confirm the fears of those who say that Synods turn churchmen and women into politicians. The truth is that this is inevitable. Debating structures such as Synods do that. The real issue is whether politics is inevitably a disreputable activity, or whether it can be an honourable activity in which concerned people seek consensus in their mutual concern for the community they serve. I take the latter view.

The House of Bishops decided, rightly or wrongly, that the best way of handling the debate was to try to manage it, and to keep it focused on the original wording of the Archdeacon of Southwark's motion. If this was to be achieved, then the Synod would have to be persuaded to resist any amendments. The Synod's Standing Orders suggested a way forward.

For the vast majority of debates, the General Synod votes as one body. The distinctions between the three Houses (of Laity, Clergy and Bishops) are ignored. It is only for resolutions that affect matters of doctrine, or when we vote on the final approval of a measure which will have the force of law, that majorities have to be recorded in each of the Houses. That said, when the time comes for any vote, a member can always request that the vote be taken by Houses. The point of doing this is that if the motion fails to get a majority in all three Houses it will fall, even if it has an overall majority in the whole Synod.

When any member intervenes to request a vote by Houses – citing the relevant Standing Order, 36(d)(iv) – the chairman will inform him or her that there needs to be at least twenty-five other members willing to stand to signify support for such a move. As there were bound to be at least forty bishops present in the General Synod, we decided to pursue this approach. The next question we had to face was whether we sprang this on the Synod or signalled our determination in advance. We decided to take the latter course, and as members read through their papers immediately before the York meetings of 1997, they were made aware that the bishops would vote against any amendment in the hope of encouraging a straight and balanced debate on the main motion. The motion, we argued, was about encouraging study and mutual listening. This was not the time to try to fix some new position.

In spite of our warning, three amendments were put down, two of which would be described as 'conservative' because they tried to strengthen the motion in the direction of the 1987 decision.

As the debate came nearer, it became clear that the press were watching closely, and that the Lesbian and Gay Christian Movement (who have never lacked courage or public relations skill) were making much of this event. Not only were they on campus and crowding the entrance to the assembly hall with their placards, but they had also managed to convey the impression that the debate was a significant step forward for their cause. It became clear to me that if the House of Bishops blocked a conservative amendment to the motion, it would be interpreted and presented as a move away from the position of 1987. I put this point to one of the people who were pressing a conservative amendment, but I came away with the impression that he genuinely thought the bishops would find it impossible to vote down what he was saying.

The big day came. The press were there in force. The Archdeacon of Southwark made a skilful and reasonable presentation of his case. He said he was asking the Synod simply to commend the document for discussion rather than to defend it. He spoke at some length on the difficulties facing many homosexual people. He claimed that there were 'many' homosexual priests and stated, with regret, that the prevailing climate since 1987 was deterring homosexuals from offering for the ministry. It seemed to me that he had said enough for the press to claim that this debate was about improving the lot of the gay community within the Church. His motion, however, was about studying a report that would still deter practising homosexuals from offering for the ministry.

The Archbishop of Canterbury spoke towards the end of the debate. His speech was noteworthy for two things. First he spoke very strongly for the traditional and – he felt – clearly biblical position on sexual activity. It was for marriage and for nowhere else. He recognized that his dogmatism might dismay some of his hearers. He did not see any inevitability in a process of discussion leading to a change of stance. In the course of his speech, however, he flagged up the likelihood of an 'international commission' within the Anglican Communion being set up to consider the issue. He said that it would be 'along the lines of the Eames Commission on the ordination of women to the episcopate'.

Whether the Archbishop realized it or not, his words

started off a hare that was going to run all over the pages of the next day's national press. The Eames Commission (named after the delightful Archbishop of Armagh) was widely regarded as the report that smoothed the way for women bishops to be accepted within the worldwide Anglican Church. Could it be that a similar commission on homosexuality would have an equally liberalizing effect on homosexual practices?

The amendments were called. Paul Oestreicher spoke with his usual eloquence to his amendment, then announced that he would not press it out of deference to the House of Bishops. The movers of the two more conservative amendments then spoke and both, to my dismay, insisted on pressing their amendments to the vote. That was when Tom Butler, who had been asked to orchestrate the bishops' parliamentary ploy, went into action. The bishops forced votes by Houses (a procedure which involves everyone laboriously walking through various doors and then reassembling to hear the results). The bishops then voted solidly against both amendments, thus defeating them. Eventually the motion was passed unamended, but with over half of the House of Laity in opposition.

The next day, however, the people of Britain were told by their newspapers that the Church of England, led by their bishops, had voted for a more relaxed attitude to homosexual practice and gay priests. The *Times* report opened as follows:

The Archbishop of Canterbury yesterday paved the way for the ordination of practising homosexuals as Church of England priests, even though he spoke out fiercely against all sexual relationships outside marriage.

Dr George Carey told the General Synod that an international commission, similar to the one which examined the issue of women priests, could be set up next year to consider 'the entire area of human sexuality'. Traditionalists said that was bound to lead eventually to the acceptance of homosexual priests and even the sanctioning of lesbian and gay marriages.

The *Daily Mail* similarly had to begin its report with a recognition that the Archbishop had signalled 'his hardening line against the gay and liberal lobbies'. Nevertheless, it continued:

> ... despite the Archbishop's lead, the 44 bishops of the synod left a chink of hope for lobbyists who want official approval for homosexual priests and equal rights for gays in the future. Voting as a block, they ensured that the synod – the Church of England's parliament – approved a motion that the current Anglican stance on homosexuality would not be 'the last word on the subject', as had been declared in 1991.

The *Guardian*'s report included comments from the Reverend Richard Kirker, the personable and skilful leader of the Lesbian and Gay Christian Movement.

> It went very well, and we hope we are at the start of a new era. The international commission is particularly welcome and we hope it achieves for us what Eames did on the ordination of women.

The *Independent* linked the vote in Synod with a government announcement on the same day concerning lowering the age of consent for homosexuals to sixteen. The two moves marked, it said, 'the advancement of gay rights'. It also picked up on the idea that the significant part of the motion was this thought about 1991 not being 'the last word on the subject'. Richard Kirker was also quoted. This time he was saying:

It represents a step forward for gay Christians seeking official acceptance at all levels of the Church.

Finally, the *Telegraph*, that most widely read of broadsheets in Anglican pews, ran a front-page story under the heading 'Church nearer to ordaining gays'. A closer reading of the short piece revealed that the evidence for this dramatic headline was, yet again, those words about 1991 being 'not the last word on the subject', plus gloomy prognostications from one Synod member about what happens when 'international commissions' are formed.

It is fair to ask whether the bishops had taken the most helpful course of action. Certainly there were many members of the Synod who, after the initial amusement of seeing forty-four bishops leap from their seats in unison, ended up feeling somewhat disgruntled at what they considered to be a stifling of genuine debate. By trying to rule out all amendments, the bishops left a motion unamended that contained a time bomb in that phrase 'not the last word'. I think the bishops were right to try to control a debate on such a significant issue. The Church of England is quick to criticize its bishops when they do not appear to give a lead. The trouble is that the synodical procedures severely limit their options. Perhaps the Archdeacon of Southwark deserves to go down in recent Church history as the man who outsmarted the House of Bishops. That said, a debate that could have been lacking in grace and shown the Synod in its worst light was avoided, and a subject that is genuinely if perplexingly important was commended to the consideration of the wider Church.

I have told this story at some length for a number of reasons. First, it gives me a chance to talk about the homosexuality issue that has been taxing the Church over the last two decades. It is my view that this is one of the issues where open and polarized debating does more harm than good. It is also important to note that while the lobbyists are skilful and much heard, the support for change in the General Synod is minimal.

My second reason for dwelling on the story is that it reveals something of the workings of General Synod and Church politics. It has become fashionable to decry Synods over the years. Back in 1970, when the Church moved into synodical government, Bishop Mervyn Stockwood lamented that it would mean 'too much sin and too much nod'! I would certainly have to admit to flaws in our procedures, and in the use we make of General Synod. I have long since come to the opinion that the majority of synodical reports – debated and sent down to be discussed by an already busy Church – have been a waste of paper and precious time. That said, if we closed down our Synods we would lose something that gives the Church at large a stake in its central affairs. The alternative would seem to be leadership by episcopal dictat, which in a nationwide community of volunteers is a formula for alienation.

The third reason for telling this story at some length is that it reveals the role played by our national press in reporting the Church's business. For a couple of years I served on the committee that arranged the business of the General Synod. I used to say that the most important group in the debating chamber were the journalists in the gallery. We needed to look at the phrasing of motions and the handling of debates with an eye on what the press might report. The speeches of members would rarely go further than the opposite wall. The interpretation of the journalists in our midst would go to the ends of the earth. The story of that debate in York 1997 would seem to bear this out.

There are, therefore, a good many shortcomings in the General Synod. That is only to be expected. It is a human institution engaged in divine affairs. It is bound to be imperfect, but I remain convinced about its value and there are times when the debates reveal genuine wisdom, profound spirituality, and the astonishing expertise in a wide range of matters to be found among the members.

I can still remember the day when I decided that I wanted to become a member of the General Synod. It was a cold, snowy winter's day in 1983 and the Synod was debating the vexed question of nuclear weapons. I was driving north up the M1 with my car radio on and the BBC was transmitting the whole debate to the nation at large. As I listened, I began to feel very proud of the dear old Church of England. The quality of the speeches, and the sense of serious listening to one another, seemed to me to be vastly superior to the efforts of the House of Commons. I felt that if I was ever offered a chance to stand for election I would take it and count it an honour.

Two years later I was given that chance. The chairman of the Guildford Diocesan Evangelical Fellowship offered to nominate me at the 1985 elections. This meant that I stood a good chance of pulling in the votes of most, if not all, of the evangelical clergy in the diocese. I did, and I was elected.

Saying this, of course, reveals that there is a strong degree of tribal voting in the synodical process. That cannot be denied. We must ask, however, whether it is obviously wrong for this to be the case. There are, broadly speaking, three main groupings to be found in the Church of England. There are the Catholics, who can be subdivided into Anglo-Catholics and Liberal Catholics. There are the evangelicals, and we have already noted that they break down (sometimes in the unfortunate sense of that word) into conservative evangelicals and open evangelicals. Finally there is a less clearly defined group between the two poles of churchmanship. Some would call them 'Liberals', but this is not always a helpful description. Some would use the term 'central', which says little other than that those so described do not belong to the other two groups. In the General Synod itself there is a fringe organization that calls itself 'the Open Synod Group'. It embraces most of those who occupy the middle ground, but just to make things complicated there are some evangelicals and Catholics who also attend their meetings.

At the beginning of each series of sessions, what used to be called the 'party meetings' take place as fringe activities. The Evangelical Group in General Synod (EGGS) has become the largest. The Catholic Group and the Open Synod Group, however, are strongly supported. There is no whipping of votes. Every individual member jealously preserves his or her right to vote according to conscience. In any case, there have sometimes been people who signed up to more than one of these 'party' groups. At the fringe meetings members consider the business that is facing them in the Synod and there is no doubt that strong suggestions are sometimes made by the leaders as to voting choices. In all my years as a member of EGGS I heard plenty of strong urgings from the platform as to how we should vote, but there was no whipping and no sanctions for the many who went their own way.

It is fashionable to decry all this. It can be seen as Christians playing politics. The truth, however, is that the Synod very accurately reflects the strength on the ground of the various traditions. The electoral system of proportional representation guarantees this. If some measure falls foul of a group in the Synod it would certainly fall foul of that group in the

Church at large. Synod is a good testing ground for the actual mind of the Church. I remember reading opinion polls that had been commissioned before the 1992 vote on the ordination of women. I remember also that the vote in Synod almost precisely matched those polls. I think the Church of England can teach the nation a thing or two about democracy.

* * *

My last memory of the General Synod was also in York. It was Tuesday the 11th July 2000. It was the last day of the sessions and the last day of that particular Synod. When we left York many of us would not return. National elections would be held for the new Synod to convene in the following November. It was a time of farewells, and I knew it was my own farewell. Mary had travelled up the day before to be with me.

The night before, I had spoken in my last debate. The subject had been on how the Church gathered and presented its statistics. Some might not feel this to be the most stimulating of subjects, but attendance figures and patterns have always interested me. I find it amazing that a Church which has seen its attendance figures dropping remorselessly over many years had never once debated the matter in its General Synod or its House of Bishops in the fifteen years I had been aware of such places. I cannot think of any business that would be so careless and cavalier about shrinking numbers of customers.

It is a tradition in the General Synod that retiring bishops are given a short tribute at their last attendance. I had often enjoyed the humour of these tributes – tongues were often in archiepiscopal cheeks – but I wondered what on earth could be thought up about me, and I wondered whether I could cope.

David Hope, Archbishop of York, was doing the honours on that day. He spoke warmly of two very distinguished members and then he turned to me. It was a very strange moment.

Finally Bishop Gavin Reid, who became a member of the General Synod in 1985 – well before being measured for a mitre. During that time he has played a prominent, significant and varied role as an ordinary member, as a member of the Standing Committee and as a member of numerous other committees and commissions of this House.

On a wider stage, our Church would have been much poorer without his vision and enthusiasm. Evangelism and mission, particularly among young people, have always been high on his agenda and he was amongst the first to recognize the urgent need to find new ways of bringing the gospel to life for the next generation. It was Gavin's amendment in the *Children in the Way* debate in 1988 that focused attention on the need to evangelize children. As a result he was asked to be a member of the subsequent working party and wrote their report *All God's Children*. It was a groundbreaking document and raised issues that still demand careful attention today.

Again it was Gavin – long before the Dome was dreamt of – who began to think of creative ways to mark the millennium. And for better or worse, once it became clear that there was going to be a Millennium Dome in Greenwich, it was Gavin more than anyone who was determined that Jesus was going to be in it. His chairmanship of the Archbishops' Millennium Advisory Group was outstanding and thanks to him, the world at large now knows that the millennium had something to do with the

Christian religion. If for no other reason, he richly deserved the OBE given to him by Her Majesty in the New Year Honours.

Bishop Michael Adie once said that Gavin Reid was the sort of speaker who could turn a debate in General Synod. The *Children in the Way* debate was only one example. Another was the debate about cohabitation in 1992. His persuasive powers have never lain in oratory or polemics. Rather they have found their strength in experience and the plain meaning of Scripture. And in the support of the woman he loves. Mary has been Gavin's greatest champion and admirer. She has shared his passionate concern for the unchurched children of our nation, and through her own work has supported and complemented Gavin in this and many other areas.

They were kind words, and Mary and I found ourselves on the receiving end of a warm ovation – not a regular experience for either of us.

'Too much sin and too much nod' perhaps, but I have always found something lovable about the General Synod. And when its members show that they actually hold you in their affections, that becomes a memory to treasure.

11

A Bishop and a Brother

'When we leave this cathedral,' said the preacher, 'I will have a brother who is a bishop and you will have a bishop who is a brother . . .'

It was Canterbury Cathedral. It was the 9th October 1992. It was my consecration as Bishop of Maidstone, and it was my brother who was preaching.

The cathedral was well filled, and everywhere I looked I could see familiar faces. People had come from the parish in Woking where I had served as an honorary curate for twenty-one years. Colleagues had come from the Church Pastoral Aid Society and from the General Synod. There were people there whom I had known from my time as a youngster in St John's, Blackheath, and they included Tony Waite, Charlie Cope and the 'young' Mr Dick who had taught me at Sunday school. There was also a remarkable turn-out from the people of the diocese whom I was going to get to know and love in the years that would follow.

And, of course, the family was there in full. They sat together in the nave of the great cathedral, with one exception. My brother Colin was the preacher and he was robed and up there in front of the large congregation, preaching in the hearing of the Archbishop of Canterbury and the man who was soon to be the Archbishop of York. It was not an everyday experience for him as someone who had given the previous thirty-two years to serving the scattered farming communities of fellside Cumbria.

It is a nice touch that when someone is about to be consecrated bishop he can choose the preacher for the service. There could have been no more fitting choice than my elder brother. All through my life he was the big brother who kept an eye on me and whom I admired. Strangely enough, we have spent far more time apart than together. In the disturbed years of the war, when the family faced a move from Scotland to London, with many uncertainties about finding a home in the strange circumstances of the time, Colin was sent to a boarding school so that his studies were not disrupted. Being younger, things were less critical in my case, so I stayed with our parents and was schooled locally. Colin and I saw each other only in school holidays. When he left school, he worked in Leeds as a voluntary helper in the famous St George's Church, and from there he went off to theological college. In spite of – or even because of – the constant separations, there was always the sense that time together was special.

Our ministries have been hugely different. Colin has committed himself to being a pastor in small, rugged communities. He has blended in and become the true 'parson' – the man of God 'there' in the midst of a community. I have worked in the world of ideas and strategies, flitting from committee to committee, planning books or missions or young people's events, and networking with others who dream dreams. Both of us, however, have shared the same vision for ministry and the same strange affection for

England's national Church and its outworking in the parish churches.

It was, therefore, very comforting for me to have my brother preaching at my consecration. It was also, as I was to find over the following years, a great advantage in a largely rural diocese to have a rural priest commending me to other rural priests. Many of the Canterbury clergy knew only that I was some middle-aged ex-whizz-kid who ran Billy Graham missions. This was hardly reassuring to them as they faced their day-to-day work in small villages and tiny congregations. For the first few years of my time in the Canterbury diocese, hardly a week passed without someone reminding me of Colin's sermon. The phrase they never forgot was the phrase that I tried to remember until the day I retired: 'a bishop who is a brother . . .'.

Those words helped me to settle for simply being myself, in spite of inhabiting the office of a bishop. I set out to be as informal as was appropriate, to let my sense of humour show, and to treat everyone I met as a friend. The last thing I wanted to be was aloof. This was not what everybody wanted. Some seem to feel that friendliness goes ill with being a 'father in God'. Some like their bishops to be a bit distant.

Perhaps being seen as more distant would have helped me on those few occasions when I had to take disciplinary steps and even bring someone's ministry to an end. I found such times very hard to cope with. To demand a priest's resignation does not merely take his or her job away – it means that the person and the family are made homeless. A friend of mine once said that the test of real leadership was the ability to take and live with unpopular decisions. My observation is that some bishops are not good at doing that, and I was one of them.

The unusual episcopal arrangements in the Canterbury diocese were helpful to the cause of being a brotherly bishop. The diocesan bishop is, and has to be, the archbishop. The problem here is that the archbishop has huge national commitments and growing international responsibilities, and he simply cannot be expected to be active as the diocesan bishop for Canterbury. To make matters more difficult from the point of view of the diocese, he has to spend most of his time living at his London address.

When George Carey came to the office in 1991, he openly acknowledged the problem. He said he would look to his two suffragan bishops (Dover and Maidstone) to give both the day-to-day and the strategic leadership. It was my good fortune to start in 1992 at the same time as a new Bishop of Dover, Richard Llewellin. He had already served as a suffragan bishop in another diocese, so he was clearly intended to be the senior of the two of us. Richard had an identical desire to be himself and to eschew a lofty and distanced style of leadership. He was determined to share his leadership role with me and with the archdeacons and the diocesan secretary. He felt that if he was to call for collaborative leadership in the parishes, it was essential to model it at the level of the senior staff of the diocese.

This had the effect of bringing me into all the action as a partner rather than a subordinate. I found Richard to be one of the humblest and most delightful people I have ever met. He would always listen to his colleagues and tended to overregard the value of our contributions. We had never met before the Archbishop brought us together, but we gelled – as did the entire senior staff – from the very first day. Staff meetings were rarely completed because we never allowed enough time on the agenda for laughter. It was not long before the bond among the senior staff was widely noticed. One clerical wag called us 'the famous five'!

When the Archbishop was able to join staff meetings – which was not as often as he would have liked – nothing changed. He clearly enjoyed the chance to join in both the planning and the banter. He never tried to draw back control to himself, and he never appeared to be simply going through the motions. There were, of course, times when he was clearly distracted by some national or overseas problem, but that was understandable. In the autumn he would sit at the table trying to follow the agenda while he doggedly signed his annual glut of Christmas cards. We would all spend an annual weekend away together, and those were times when George Carey could catch up with the big picture as far as the diocese was concerned and contribute his thoughts to plans ahead. Those were also the times when we could see how much he, and his wife Eileen, loved party games.

I dare to think that the accident of personalities and the strange nature of the diocese meant that Canterbury was able to model a different sort of episcopacy from any other diocese in the country. Neither Richard nor myself were in the House of Lords. We were not given large cars or chauffeurs or full-time chaplains. The support arrangements for us were modest. We worked as a team and we worked within a team. People knew that we were easy to contact and to see. In addition, the bishops and archdeacons worked through a schedule of parish visits where we would stay for the best part of a day in a parish or benefice, getting the chance to meet and talk with clergy and lay leaders and seeing the issues they faced for ourselves. The unobtrusive presidency of the Archbishop, and his obvious enjoyment of his visits to the diocese, also made it easier for Richard and me to be leaders who saw ourselves as working alongside people rather than over them.

I think that the enforced modesty of our episcopal life-style had a good effect on morale, and morale was a key factor in the difficult times we had to face. The work of clergy in rural parishes can be very lonely. The Canterbury diocese had very few large congregations or prosperous sub-urban parishes. I remember calculating that 60 per cent of our parishes had a usual Sunday attendance of under fifty people, while 40 per cent drew fewer than twenty-five. That was not a comment on poor levels of ministry, but on the size of the communities those churches served. Clergy would often have responsibility for two, three or four churches linked together.

The problem in these 'multi-parish benefices' is often that parishioners maintain the same expectations of their parish priests as were held when each village had its own vicar. As if that was not difficult enough, the ways of the Church of England often mean that rural clergy are expected to chair church council meetings and other committees in each one of their parishes. There are ways of uniting parishes to prune the committees, but these are often rejected because the parish-ioners (with some good reason) prefer to see their church iden-tified with the community rather than the team of parishes. They have an instinct that the clergy are there for the benefit of the churches and not the churches for the benefit of the clergy.

Although I had never ministered in such circumstances, I knew from my consultancy work with CPAS, and also from my brother's experience, just how demanding and even depressing it can be to be a country vicar. The outside world looks on at the village settings and thinks that these men and women have an idyllic existence, but nothing could be further from the truth.

As the years have progressed the problems have mounted. In the new competitive philosophy about education, the village primary school (where it still exists) can be targeted by parents over a wide area wanting to exercise their choice to send their children to a happy school in safe surroundings. The visit from the vicar does little in such schools to build up community and make links to Sunday ministry, because the schoolchildren disperse at the end of the day to other neighbourhoods.

The poor state of public transport means that, unless they are driven around by ever-available parents, children and young people cannot easily be brought together for church activities. It also means that the clergy have to drive long distances in their cars, often getting too little in terms of expenses from overstretched church councils.

Then there are things like heating bills. Some of the coldest places on earth can be rural churches in the winter. A congregation of eight people with an elderly organist wrestling with a temperamental organ, plus a vicar who has to rush off to the next village immediately after the service, and all in a damp and chilly building, is hardly likely to be an attractive prospect to anyone other than the most dedicated believer.

When one is a vicar facing these sorts of problems, to say nothing of living on a modest stipend, it is hardly reassuring to see your diocesan bishop being chauffeur-driven to the front door in a large car. I feel that the discrepancy in lifestyles between bishops and clergy is too much, especially at a time when local congregations are under constant pressure to pay the cost of their clergy and to keep their ancient buildings intact. Every now and then, the press or some members of parliament howl in protest at the published levels of working expenses for our bishops. Some of the indignation is misplaced, as the figures cited as 'expenses' are boosted far more by the salaries of essential staff than by large amounts of wining and dining. Some of the indignation, however, is rightly expressed. It is no defence to point out that the money comes from the Church Commissioners rather than the parishes. That is true, but it only means that the funds thus directed are not available to help the poorer parishes and dioceses.

I would want to suggest that the Canterbury episcopal model has lessons to teach the Church at large. At several levels of its activity, the Church of England is cutting suits that are larger than the available cloth.

In 1994 the Canterbury senior staff – along with every equivalent group throughout the Church of England – had to face an unexpected and deeply threatening challenge. We learned that the Church Commissioners, at a time when markets were fragile, had lost about £800 million of the Church's assets. The initial reaction coming from the Commissioners was that the Church of England would have to move quickly from being an organization highly subsidized from the centre to one that would have to pay its way in practically every one of its parishes. I was told that only a year or so before I came to the diocese the Church Commissioners' contribution towards the pay of Canterbury's ministers was near to £1 million. We faced the prospect of receiving nothing at all within a very few years. It was hard to see how this would be possible.

The Archbishop joined us for a weekend in a French retreat house and there we started to hammer out a response to the circumstances. As we thought about it, we could see that we had not one but two crises. There was the money question, but there was also a looming ministry shortfall. In 1911, when the national population stood at 34 million, the Church was served by 20,086 full-time, paid clergy. In 1938, when the population stood at 38.4 million, the number of serving clergy had dropped to 17,139. When I was ordained the clergy numbers were down to around 16,000. In the closing years of my time in Canterbury, the nation's population was up by another 10 million or so on the 1938 figures, but the number of full-time, paid clergy was dropping towards the 9,000 mark.

It was clear to us, as we tried to plan ahead, that we would have to prepare the diocese for both these shortfalls. We would have to develop a new approach to giving and funding our operations, and we would have to find a radical strategy for ministry. The days when congregations could expect their clergy to do it all for them were long gone, and even in the recent times when readers (the strange name we use for lay-people trained and licensed to lead services and preach) were far more prominent, we were still not going to meet the challenges. Either we would have to close churches, or we would have to create a new ministry culture where Christian people took the responsibility to run their local churches and maintain regular congregational worship. In this new culture, the ordained clergy would have to act more as trainers and over-seers and less as all-sufficient pastors. Drawing on the experience of other dioceses such as Gloucester, and remembering a long disregarded but prophetic report by Canon John Tiller, we worked out a strategy document for the diocese.

At this point we had to learn some uncomfortable lessons. Our report, which we simply called *The Future*, set out a policy for money and ministry. Richard (and I supported him in this) believed that the diocese needed a strong and clear lead. We felt that once we had run this past the rural deans we could launch it on the diocese in a series of meetings built round the traditional archdeacon's visitations, which take place each year shortly after Easter. We sent draft copies of the report to the rural deans and arranged a meeting. It was to prove a difficult occasion.

For various reasons, the rural deans did not warm to what we were proposing or to the way in which we were intending to push through with our plans. They could see that the report envisaged a different job description for a priest which could be summed up in a complaint that some of them raised, and which we were to hear many times over: 'I was ordained to be a pastor, not a manager.'

They did not like the prescriptive way in which we had written the document. They said, with some justification, that it did not read like a discussion paper. It came over as a plan of action – a plan cooked up by an élite group without any consultation. They told us that introductory talks at the forthcoming archdeacon's visitations would not be enough. There would need to be a round of deanery meetings where people could have a chance to raise their questions and criticisms. They told us that the senior staff would have to alter their diaries and take part in all these deanery meetings to hear people's concerns for themselves.

With hindsight, I think what they were really saying was, 'If you bishops really want to act like brothers, then you need to think alongside us and not over our heads.' I think they were right. It was a salutary lesson for Richard and myself.

Leadership in the Church of England is a very difficult business. Bishops and archdeacons have none of the dynamics of 'bosses' over 'workforce'. The vast majority of those who work for the Church's cause are lay volunteers. There can be no hiring and firing in such circumstances. When it comes to the clergy, the majority of those in post have the freehold, which again means that the bishop can do little about them unless they commit adultery! If bishops want to make things happen in the sprawling community of volunteers that we call the Church of England, they have to find ways of making that community want to own what is being proposed. The alternative (and it happens frequently) is that bishops dream up and announce bright new initiatives, and everyone smiles and keeps their heads down until the bishop thinks of something else. As Archbishop John Habgood once put it, 'He who leads when no one is following is merely going on a walk.' Peter Nott, formerly Bishop of Norwich, put it another way: 'In our diocese the secret of leadership is to find out which way people are wanting to go, and place yourself in front of them!'

Thus it was that Richard and I, plus our archdeacons Michael Till and Patrick Evans, and David Kemp our diocesan secretary, spent the summer of 1994 trailing round from one meeting to another discussing our proposals and being forced to listen to fair and unfair criticisms. There was some tough talking. The exercise culminated in the issuing of another report, which set out the main things that we felt we had heard, modified our proposals where necessary and listed resolutions to be placed before the Diocesan Synod. Those resolutions highlighted the main concerns in our two reports and called for their implementation.

The first of the resolutions committed us to the ideal of maintaining worship and witness 'in every parish and neighbourhood, working in partnership with other churches wherever this is possible'.

The second supported the principle of 'ministry teams' in every church in the diocese. A ministry team (we later called them 'ministry leadership teams') consisted of a group of people who were felt by the clergy and people of a church to be the obvious people to look to for leadership. They would include the priest-in-charge, backed by others felt to have pastoral, teaching, liturgical and strategic skills.

The aim here was to identify such people, get them into service, and provide such training as they needed *while* they were ministering and not *before*. The third resolution thus called for 'easily accessible, flexible, practical and theological training to be made available to resource the emerging ministry teams'. This was something new in the way that the Church of England has approached ministry. In the past we have always trained ministers (lay or clerical) before licensing them to engage in regular ministry. Our proposals were that those judged to have the gifts should be put to work, under guidance, from the start and that training should be given 'on the job'.

Other resolutions called for a group to explore a 'local non-stipendiary ministry' scheme, approved a new way of raising and handling diocesan monies, called parishes and benefices to meet the cash costs of their stipendiary clergy, and recognized that there would always be needy parishes needing financial help from the rest of the diocese.

All the proposals met with overwhelming support from the Synod. Making something actually happen in the light of these resolutions, however, was a slow and laborious process. It proved to be deeply threatening to some of the clergy, and understandably so. They had been trained to be one-man-band ministers. Frequently in my training college days I would hear the phrase 'and when you get your own parish'. Some of our language gives the game away. It is not uncommon to speak of 'Harry Walker's congregation' when we actually

mean the congregation that Harry Walker is supposed to
serve. There have always been a few clergy who have needed to
be needed and who, in a subtle way, have made their service
indispensable.

For centuries the Church of England has had a plentiful
supply of clergy on the cheap. The prevailing culture of ministry was one where the clergy were the initiators of ministry
and the laity were the receivers. It may seem a flattering
scenario for the parish priest, but it was never truly possible in
one parish to meet all the pastoral needs of the parishioners.
In today's Church, with far fewer clergy, it is impossible to
work in large parishes or multi-parish benefices on a one-man
ministry basis. Unless the culture is changed, and the expectations on and of our clergy change also, we have a formula for
burnt-out clergy and dwindling congregations.

It was not long before I found the expectations placed on
our bishops to be equally unrealistic. I moved into the
Bishop's House a few weeks before I was consecrated. I found
a pile of forms waiting for my signature. I could not sign them
until I had been 'done'. The forms were all about episcopal
permission for laypeople to assist with the distribution of the
elements at Communion services. The more I thought about
it, the more ridiculous it seemed. There I was, brand new to
the area, without a clue about the names in front of me. And
what was the task for which the bishop's intervention was
necessary? It was to pass along a row of people, reverently and
unobtrusively, and to give a portion of bread or wine, while
repeating set phrases.

I remember thinking: does this really need a bishop's permission? I also remember musing on the thought that a bishop
was needed before someone could repeat set phrases at a
Communion service, but not in the case of Sunday school

teachers who would be entrusted to teach the faith to new generations of human beings. No ministry is more important than that, but it is not considered important enough to bother a bishop.

Also on my desk was a letter from a vicar who was desperate for me to come and consecrate an extension to his graveyard as soon as possible. Apparently all the plots were used up and people were dying with monotonous regularity. I was tempted to write back urging him to start a healing ministry, at least until I was consecrated. When the day came for me to conduct that service, I found it almost incomprehensible. It was partly legal, with official plans and documents to sign, and partly a melancholic beating of the bounds of the new burial patch with variants of the same prayer at every turn. I could not help thinking that bishops should have better things to do.

The two matters just mentioned, however, highlight the problem of what we expect from our bishops. They are wheeled out to consecrate and dedicate memorial windows and other immovable objects that take a congregation's fancy. They are expected to give endless talks, and to write calming answers to irate non-attenders who think that the duty minister at the local crematorium (over whom he has no control) was insensitive. They are expected to come up with slick answers for some cub reporter who rings up and expects the subject of in-vitro fertilization to be covered in one paragraph. They are required to read endless papers from the General Synod or the House of Bishops, to be ahead of the game when it comes to race awareness or child protection matters, and to negotiate regular hassles where five parishes are about to be asked to manage with three vicars. And all this is to say nothing of things that make sense, such as preaching and teaching, caring for the clergy, licensing and instituting new incumbents, conducting confirmations, making pastoral visits to parishes and to schools, prisons and factories, chairing committees and working groups, and interviewing candidates for new appointments. Few things can create more havoc than a bad parochial appointment.

I found that I was expected to be a leader at the same time as being a sort of ritual odd-job man. There were many occasions when I described myself as 'doing a Prince Philip', which meant being shown round places and people and looking interested. I was constantly on the go and yet I was also expected to be a thinker, a reflector, an intercessor and the pastor of last resort. I was expected to produce talks, sermons or addresses on about 250 occasions a year, all of which required preparation beforehand, and all of which would have to be delivered under the pressure of people expecting me to be 'good'.

And I would do it all again, but I kept feeling, and I still feel, that the total effect of all these demands is that innovation is extremely hard and that the odds favour the continuation of the status quo. Every year in July I would have a bad-tempered two days. That was the time when we would draw up the diary for the next year. I would sit beside my part-time chaplain, my secretary and my wife and watch another year of my life being promised away as we went through the pile of requests and the lists from Diocesan House. The problem here was that all these invitations and committee dates were based on prevailing assumptions about my job. I remember once reading some good advice. It was that you need to be sure of your own agenda, because if this is not the case, other people have agendas for you, and you will end up being what other people want you to be. I think I failed to impose my own vision on the job.

There is, however, another side to this lament about being at everyone's beck and call. One needs to remember that the person everyone is calling on and pulling into their own agendas is a bishop – someone who is totally identified with the cause of Christ. To speak at a Rotary, to attend a high sheriff's lunch, to preach at a civic service, to give out the prizes at the annual school prizegiving, to agree to an interview on local radio, to write a monthly column in the local newspaper, to open a new health centre, to dedicate a new bridge in the county town and a new wing in the local hospice – all these things are indicators that the community still feels that the Church is significant. They are opportunities to keep the memory of Christ alive.

After I had been in office for a year or so, I went to see the mayor of Maidstone. I said that I wanted to do something that would bring churches and local leadership together. We talked over options and ended up with the idea of holding an exploratory breakfast and inviting the great and the good of the town to come together. The Archbishop kindly funded this event and, appropriately, we met in a building that was formerly one of the palaces used by medieval archbishops as they travelled to and from Canterbury. The palace, now owned by the local authority, had a magnificent dining hall and good catering facilities.

That was the start of a pattern of regular 'Bishop's Breakfasts' in Maidstone. We held three a year in the palace, and some time later the town's chief executive told me that they had become among the most important fixtures in the civic calendar. Every mayor supported the breakfasts, which were also attended by local members of parliament, key people in the town and county councils, the local chief of police and head of the fire service, bank managers, school heads, the proprietor of the *Kent Messenger* newspaper chain, the chief executive of the local health trust and many more. I invited key ministers from the different local denominations, but I restricted clergy numbers deliberately so as not to over-balance things.

We would meet at 7.45, sit down to a cooked breakfast, and then I would introduce a speaker who would talk about matters of a spiritual, moral or social significance. The pattern developed of eating and chatting for half an hour, then listening to the speaker for twenty minutes, followed by questions and open discussion. Just before 9.00 I would try to sum up, putting a gentle Christian gloss on things and sending folk on their various ways. It gave me an opportunity to exercise some leadership in the affairs of the community at large. It was modest, but it was recognized.

We never had fewer than forty present and at my final breakfast over seventy attended. I spoke about the importance of the *story* of Christ in our cultural history. I argued that the story had been the inspiration to many people and the main stimulus for most of our traditional social values. I pointed out that a very high percentage of those who engaged in voluntary services and in the caring professions did so from Christian motivations. I suggested that the story needed to continue as the main value-shaping influence in our culture. It was like the gold standard behind a currency. Whether one was a believer or stood apart, I suggested that the social value of the story needed to be recognized and that a fair wind needed to be given in our communities to those who made the story known.

They listened well and there seemed to be an openness to

what I was saying. I suppose they realized that, six days before my retirement, this was my last word to the movers and shakers in the county town. After some open discussion, the mayor stood up and said that the breakfasts had changed the nature of civic life in Maidstone. To my surprise he then handed me a silver salver on which was inscribed:

> Rt Rev. GAVIN REID OBE
> *Bishop of Maidstone*
> *1992–2000*
> *from his friends of the*
> *Bishop's Breakfasts*
> *9th October 2000*

Whether or not the breakfasts changed the nature of Maidstone's civic life, they certainly proved to me that the Church of England, and especially its bishops, can still play a significant part in public affairs. I never felt that I was intruding or interfering. I felt that my modest contribution was welcomed and indeed helped to demonstrate that there was such a thing as a community in the town. One of the problems with the Churches is that they are so clear about their own problems that they can lose sight of the fact that all sections of the community are facing problems. They can be so convinced about being minority groups that they fail to realize that there are no majority groups. The effects of fragmentation and the privatization of choices can be seen on all sides, be it a shortage of volunteers to lead Scout groups or the urge of the alienated to scrawl graffiti on walls. The people who take up local politics and involve themselves in the affairs of the community are usually those who want to see others coming together and taking responsibility for what happens outside their front doors. To such people the Churches are a relative success story in a world of disappointments.

This was certainly the line taken by the Conservative administration on the Kent County Council. Towards the end of my time in Maidstone the bishops and archdeacons in the Dioceses of Canterbury and Rochester were being invited to meetings with key county executives to review community issues. We were told that local and county authorities increasingly relied on partnerships with voluntary agencies if social policy was to be delivered. We were also told that the Churches were recognized as the biggest players when it came to voluntary effort.

All this would fall, it seems to me, within the area described in the Bible as 'the kingdom of God'. The basic understanding behind the Lord's Prayer is that the 'earth' (not just the Church) needs God's kingdom to come and his will to be done. When this is realized, one can see how often the Church thinks in dimensions that are too constricted. There is a danger with missionary thinking that is only focused on congregational growth, and the danger is that of forgetting that God is concerned for, and at work in, the world at large. Christians are meant to be witnesses to the values of heaven in a world that, at times, can be more like hell. St Paul was clear that people in public office were serving the causes of God. The more they are reminded of that, and the more they are helped to do that, the better.

If I did not see it before, eight years as the Bishop of Maidstone convinced me that England needs to have a Christian Church established firmly in its midst, and, as it already has one officially, this is not the time for that Church to want to turn away and bury itself in blinkered domesticity. The day for disestablishment is the day when the nation asks us to go. Until it says so we should consider ourselves wanted.

All this is not to say that bishops should ignore things like church attendance levels. I personally took them very seriously. Every autumn, in common with other dioceses, we did head counts in our churches to determine what we called 'usual Sunday attendance' (USA) figures. Those figures were one of the factors that enabled us to determine what each parish would be asked to pay into the central kitty to keep the diocesan ship afloat. It was well known that the head count was related to this 'parish share' or 'quota', and it is equally well known that the figures sent in from the parishes are hardly likely to be exaggerated!

The USA figures, therefore, were a far from accurate assessment of the strength in the parishes. For one thing, they did not include the numbers present in church under eighteen years of age. Nevertheless, they were the only figures we collected year on year, and the same procedures were used each year to collect them. They had value as indicators of whether churches were growing or shrinking. I remember looking at the USA returns in the autumn of 1993 and realizing with a jolt that in one year we were down by about 500. I checked back to the figures for 1991 and 1992 and saw that this sort of decline was recorded in those years also. In some four years attendances had dropped from the region of 16,000 on any given Sunday to around 14,000. I phoned Richard Llewellin late in the evening to say that unless we could stop the rot there were going to be serious developments within the next few years. Richard did not seem to feel the same sort of alarm, but he admitted the next day that thoughts on the problem had kept him awake that night.

Mission-related matters were part of my portfolio, so I felt that I had to start making clergy and lay leaders conscious of this serious pattern of decline. As I have already remarked, it is a singular fact that very little direct talking goes on about attendance levels in the Church of England. It seems fashionable to put on a lofty expression and claim to be above such sordid concerns. 'Evangelism,' I have often been told, 'is far more than mere bottoms on pews.'

I found this a very difficult issue to raise in a way that would lead to positive thinking. The truth is that very many clergy are only too aware of fighting what others would call a losing battle. Many have a sense of failure and even guilt. A bishop chuntering on about losing 400 to 500 worshippers a year is hardly going to be good for morale. Having said that, relatively few churches seem to be prepared to change what they do on Sundays in order to improve their attendance levels. One of the most serious failings of the Church of England is that for the last thirty years we have known that informal Family Services will bring fresh faces into our churches, and yet very many congregations refuse to hold them, or at the most offer only one such service a month. Great play is made about the Eucharist being the supreme act of worship for the Christian, which is undoubtedly the case, but this is no argument for ruling out other forms of worship.

It is a remarkable fact that in the years since 1950 a graph would show that at the same time as the numbers of confirmations have fallen steadily, the numbers of churches offering only eucharistic worship on a Sunday morning have risen equally steadily. I decided to champion the cause of non-eucharistic, all-age services whenever I spoke to clergy and church councils.

When the USA figures for 1994 came through, they showed that the decline was continuing although the rate of decline

had slowed. As I studied them, however, I became aware of a
number of congregations that were bucking the trend. With
this in mind, I went back to the figures for the previous two
years and was able to detect a number of churches which had
revealed growth over all three years. I invited clergy from some
of these churches to come and meet Richard Llewellin and
myself. As they talked about what they were doing, we were
able to see a number of common factors, in spite of the fact
that they represented all shades of churchmanship. Not surprisingly, one factor was that they were actually trying to
grow! Another was that they were all trying to build bridges
into their communities. A third factor was that they offered a
variety of worship experiences – they were not Eucharist-only
churches. A fourth factor they seemed to have in common was
that they took teaching and preaching seriously.

Soon after meeting with these clergy I had to give a presi-
dential address at our Diocesan Synod. Because I had discovered these growing parishes, I decided that I could talk about
numbers without depressing people. We were able to show
that the trend could be bucked and that there were lessons to
learn. I duly gave the address and took every opportunity
thereafter to pass on this message.

Whether the efforts of the senior staff to talk numbers and
to discuss possibilities for growth was the reason for a change
in our attendance patterns, I shall never know. The fact
remains that for the next six years our attendance levels
stopped falling. In 1995 the numbers were up, and in the six
years that followed we alternated between years of slight
losses and years of slight gains.

What we also began to realize as we studied the figures was
that people were changing their patterns of worship. One of
our parish priests, the Reverend Anthea Williams, conducted

a survey of her village congregations and noted that, although the attendance figures each week varied little, the actual individuals who attended differed from week to week. At the same time as this was being studied in other parts of the country, she discovered that while her USA was something like fifty, her pool of regular worshippers was more than twice that number. Wider testing in the diocese revealed the same phenomenon. As a rule of thumb we could say that on any given Sunday only about 40 per cent of our 'regular' worshippers were in church. The implications of this nationally are immense. Much play is made in the media of Church of England numbers dropping below the million mark. Those figures are based on USA returns. The truth is likely to be that over two million people attend our parish churches with a degree of regularity.

This phenomenon of irregular regularity can be interpreted in totally different ways. It can be seen positively as an indication that Christianity, as measured by church attendance, is far stronger than many realize. This is true and it is also very important. Commentators and columnists are prone to talk about the fast-emptying pews of the churches and to imply that the Church is past its sell-by date. The facts do not fully support their pessimism. On the other hand, the church attendance patterns can be seen in a more sobering light. They could be pointers to declining levels of commitment. For some time I have felt that, like everyone else, Christians are being infected with the consumer mind-set of our times. According to this mind-set, a church service is simply one option among others facing each person on a choice-filled Sunday. By not going to church one is simply exercising one's right to make choices, and that right is more important than God's right to your worship.

A further unpalatable interpretation of the phenomenon is that our church services are simply not attractive and compelling enough. Whether we want to admit to this or not, the fact is that churches are in a very competitive world. If we do not appear attractive, then we simply will not attract.

It is small wonder, in the light of an overall appearance of decline, that many of the clergy and their congregations are running on low levels of morale. One thing I was always clear about is that morale is important. In my second curacy, with the struggling little congregation in riverside Essex, I soon realized that the faithful were finding that 'church' was hard work and bad news. We needed to laugh and to see some things working well.

One of my heroes is Field Marshall Montgomery, who knew the importance of creating confidence and high morale if an army was to fight well. I kept a little list in my diary of 'The Tasks of a Bishop'. One of those tasks was:

To create atmospheres
(i)   Good morale
(ii)   A desire for holiness
(iii)   A passion for souls

It is easy to write things in diaries. I found it harder to work out how to actually lift levels of morale. One of the conclusions I came to was that much had to depend on my own bearing. It was important to be positive and cheerful and to make this clear. I found that confirmations and the institutions of new clergy were important occasions for lifting people's spirits. Those services are occasions when the bishop is literally in charge and controls the mood. I knew that I had to project confidence and good humour on such occasions.

We would always have larger than usual attendances, so that also helped to create a congregational sense of wellbeing. I think that institutions were my favourite services. These were the services where new vicars were launched on their ministries, and in Canterbury we always tried to link the ministry of the clergy to that of the laity. Thus an institution was a time when everyone could resolve to serve God with greater faithfulness in the days ahead.

One of the great things about institutions was that I worked in tandem with Patrick Evans, the Archdeacon of Maidstone, a man who was larger than life in just about every aspect. He is one of those people who just make you feel better because he is there! On one occasion he and I were to license Lindsey Hammond to be priest-in-charge of a tiny village church. He was already the priest-in-charge of several other adjacent parishes on the edge of Romney Marsh, and he was being asked to take on a further responsibility. For some reason, however, I turned up without the all-important legal documents which not only have to be given to the new priest but also have to be read out in front of the whole congregation.

There was no time to send someone back to Bishop's House for the papers. There was only one thing to do. Patrick and I searched the vestry and found one remaining piece of A4 paper, which was the right size. I knelt down with a pencil – there was no chair in the vestry – and together we dreamed up a wording that sounded appropriately legal. I folded it in three to look like the normal licence, and when the time came, with Lindsey solemnly kneeling in front of me (and working hard to keep a straight face), I read out the phoney document. Nobody realized, and one of the reasons for this was that – as Patrick and I found afterwards – we had virtually got it right, almost word for word! Lindsey told me later that he had framed our home-made licence and hung it on some appropriate wall. I hasten to add that the real licence was in the post the following day.

In the Canterbury diocese we also had another morale-boosting option open to us, and that was the Archbishop himself. It was true that he had made it clear he could not be an active diocesan to us, but he became an active missioner. Every year he would make two or three visits to parishes, or groups of parishes, to conduct a teaching mission. Those missions were greatly appreciated and always had the by-product of leaving the parishes feeling good about having the Archbishop and his wife all to themselves for several days. He usually arrived looking understandably tired, and usually left us looking invigorated. It would appear that his morale also took a boost from these missions.

* * *

The year after we had learned of the huge losses sustained by the Church Commissioners, I talked to the editor of our diocesan newspaper and we decided to launch a poll to find out the ten most popular hymns in the diocese. We linked the poll to a 'Songs of Praise' service in the cathedral where we would all gather to sing our favourites. I felt that there were few things more likely to lift morale and true up our perspectives than to bring the congregations together to sing the great hymns of the faith. When the day came for the service, none of us had any idea whether many people would turn up or not. What I found when I arrived at the cathedral was a huge crowd pouring through the doors and packing the nave. It was a great service and we repeated it every year.

When it was known that I would be retiring in the autumn of 2000, I asked if we could time the 'Songs of Praise' service to coincide with my farewell. Mary and I chose hymns that were linked to particular moments in our life and we introduced them to the large congregation. I helped plan the service, but there was one thing that I did not know about.

One of the items I wanted everybody to sing was a children's chorus that Mary and I had both sung in the Sunday school where we had first met. When we arrived for the service we found that the staff and children of my favourite school were all there, primed to sing the chorus first and then to get everyone to join in.

St Stephen's School is in Tovil, a suburb of Maidstone where there are many residents who experience more than their fair share of social deprivation. Many of the children in the school come from broken homes. Led by a superb head, with a courageous and committed staff, the school is a beacon in the community. It is, quite simply, the happiest school I have ever visited. In one of my monthly articles in the *Kent Messenger* I spoke about their Nativity play one year and called the school a place where it is always Christmas.

So there they were, waving ribbons and standing proudly in front of over a thousand people in the great cathedral. And they sang the words which I learned as a child and which have helped me all through my life:

> Turn your eyes upon Jesus,
> Look full in his wonderful face.
> And the things of earth will grow strangely dim
> In the light of his glory and grace!

As Mary and I drove out of the cathedral gates after the
service, and as the finality of our retirement began to dawn on
us, we could not have been better equipped than to carry with
us the memory of those children, and the song that they had
turned up to sing.

12

Doctors in the House

'Your Grace,' interjected the bishop, sitting near the back of the large room where a meeting of the House of Bishops was taking place. 'I wonder if I am the only person here who feels as if I'm travelling on a train going where I don't want to go, and wondering how I can get off?'

The subject was liturgical revision and we were being briefed by the Bishop of Salisbury on something which escapes me, except that it is a fair bet that it was complicated and dated back to third-century usage. From 1995 to 2000 liturgical revision was the biggest show in town as far as the General Synod and the House of Bishops were concerned. The astonishing thing is that very early in George Carey's tenure of office he took part in a discussion with the General Synod's Standing Committee to identify what members thought were the Church's priorities for the 1990s. Liturgical revision hardly got a mention.

The perplexed bishop who wanted to find a way to get off the train was not alone in his feelings that there were better things to do. I remember his question, and to spare his blushes I shall not mention his name. What I also remember is that he did not get an answer. There were chuckles, a smiling nod from the Archbishop in the chair, and we carried on with the liturgical agenda.

'So there *is* no way we can get off,' he muttered sadly.

I have never been sure why we had to replace the Alternative Service Book (ASB). I do know that when it was approved in 1980, for use alongside *The Book of Common Prayer*, the approval was only for a period of ten years. In 1985 I remember a debate in the General Synod to review the fortunes and future of what was then, still, the new book. The overwhelming feeling was that it would be too soon to be introducing further changes in 1990, so the book was given further approval until 2000. Somehow or other, the die was cast for a major liturgical exercise in the late 1990s and, like Everest, we climbed it because it was there.

The new book is a remarkable achievement, but I am not sure that we got it right. I think it has a better Eucharist and a better Psalter, but I am at a loss to see anything else that significantly improves on the ASB. It has all the marks of composition by people whose major concern is eucharistic worship. The material on offer for different forms of Communion service overbalances all the other material – 180 pages in all. The replacements for Morning and Evening Prayer seem to me to be lacking in shape and purpose. The Baptism and Confirmation services seem to work on the principle that one should never say three words when eight are possible. The once-promised inclusion of an order for a Family Service has been set aside and the reader is given a sort of 'do-it-yourself kit' for putting together 'A Service of the Word' which may or may not be adapted for all-age worship.

I campaigned for the inclusion of a Family Service, not to tie the hands of those clergy who have put their own forms of service together, but to give a clear signal of legitimacy for this form of worship and hopefully to offer some good practice from the talented liturgists available to the Liturgical Commission. On one occasion, either in the General Synod itself or in the House of Bishops (I cannot remember which, but the subject matter constantly ping-ponged from one to the other), I thought that the Bishop of Salisbury had assured me that a Family Service would be included in the new book – indeed, that there might even be two forms of service.

In Monica Furlong's excellent book *CofE: The State It's In*, she includes the transcript of an interview with the Archbishop of Canterbury. In the course of the interview he says,

> I hope the new services are going to give the Church one or two forms of family worship that people can use, which will be good forms in themselves, because I think the family service is very much a growth area.[1]

Clearly, the Archbishop had a similar understanding to me on this matter. Late in the day the group responsible for steering through the new book, to be known as *Common Worship*, took the view that Family Services did not lend themselves to being enshrined in a book intended for use over a number of years. In spite of pleas to reconsider from the floor of the Synod, that was the end of it.

Quite apart from the merits or otherwise of the new book, there is the whole question of the cost of introducing it. When *Common Worship* was published, it was backed with a legislative move against the ASB. After 2000, it would no longer be legal tender as far as liturgy was concerned. While a typical

---

[1] M. Furlong, *CofE: The State It's In* (Hodder & Stoughton, 2000), p. 165.

Anglican compromise was arrived at to allow bishops to grant short-term stays of execution in particular cases, the fact of the matter was that the parishes had to buy a completely new set of worship materials. They did not necessarily have to buy the book itself – in Canterbury we advised against that – but they had to spend out on booklet versions of the various services or pay for their own local versions of the new services to be produced. I hate to think how much money was sucked out of parish coffers for this changeover at the very time when the parishes were feeling the harsher financial realities after the Church Commissioners debacle.

The book itself is more of a specialist's resource book than a people's book, and I feel there is something sadly significant about that. To be frank, it is not about *common* worship. It is now taken for granted that the day is past when the rank-and-file believer can have, and can use at home, a compact book that he or she can also take to church. I regret that. A further book has been produced for the individual believer to use for daily prayer. It is so full of options and alternatives, however, that it reminds me of a railway timetable!

Now I am retired and more frequently in the pew on a Sunday, it is salutary to have to experience using *Common Worship*. Even in the booklet form which my local church uses, following the Eucharist requires constant announcements of page numbers and darting to and fro over the various sections. There are no paragraph numbers and the print is small and sanserif, which I was told in my publishing days was fine for display purposes, but less easy on the eye for continuous reading. The only plus, to my mind, is that once one has learned how to dodge around all the options, the Eucharist is a richer and better service than was offered by the ASB.

Tied in with the new book is the new lectionary. This moves

away from the approach of the ASB, which sought to impose themes on every Sunday and dig out scriptures to match the themes. The new lectionary works on the basis of consecutive readings through books of the Bible so that worshippers coming every Sunday can have a better idea of the flow of thought. It is ironic that this has surfaced at the very time when the Church has discovered that its members do not attend on consecutive Sundays.

It may well be that I have become grumpy in my old age, but assuming for the moment that my criticisms are justified, who should take the blame for all this? The answer is rather uncomfortable, because the answer is, partly, *me*. I was a member of the House of Bishops when all these changes were taking place.

While everything in the new book had to survive the continuous scrutiny of the General Synod, the House of Bishops had a key role in the process. Liturgy enshrines the doctrine of the Church and that, ultimately, is bishops' business. Before General Synod could give final approval to any of the book's contents, the House of Bishops had to pronounce its satisfaction with what was on offer.

The responsibility, therefore, cannot be laid at the door of the Bishop of Salisbury's Liturgical Commission, and certainly not with the Bishop of Salisbury himself, who carried out the tortuous task assigned to him with industry, skill, humour and charm. His commission ultimately had a servant role in the exercise. Whether or not it wanted to press anything through the House, the fact is that the bishops are all able and intelligent men and there is no way that they could be easily pressurized. The truth, I believe, was not that the Liturgical Commission pressurized the bishops. The truth is that the bishops are permanently pressurized through the unbearable weight of the business before them. 'Weight' is the right word to use. I weighed my paperwork for the three meetings of the House in 1999 and it came to exactly half a stone on the bathroom scales. And some of the papers were missing!

I have already pointed out how the Ministry Division has ended up with so much power in its possession. The whole question of the selection and training of new ministers, the monitoring of colleges and the maintenance of standards, and the continuous reflection on the working conditions of the clergy, is a massive one. It requires an immense amount of work and the development of a great deal of expertise. Ministry, however, is only one of a host of agendas that the House of Bishops has to consider and keep under review. There is only one way to do it, and that is to entrust ecclesiastical civil servants to do it for you. What soon happens, however, is that your civil servants are so far ahead of you with regard to their areas of concern that you cannot easily catch up. The only other alternative is to 'trust them to get on with it'.

The same dynamics were in play regarding liturgical revision in the 1990s. There is no way that the House of Bishops could sit down and produce effective liturgy. The subject not only requires an understanding of the nature and dynamics of public worship, it also requires awareness of liturgical developments around the world and through the ages. Liturgy is also an academic discipline and there are experts in existence, and somewhere in the mix there is the need for poets. What happens, therefore, is that the bishops subcontract this area to the specialists who – without deliberate mischief – are soon running rings round their taskmasters.

With hindsight, I feel the bishops could have prepared a brief for the Liturgical Commission, setting out their understanding of the cultural and missionary situation in the country. From that appreciation of the situation the liturgical needs of what has to be a missionary Church could have been identified. I am not aware that the House, or the General Synod, ever did that. The commission itself may have worked to its own understandings of what was needed, but that should not have been its business. Years ago Alan Stibbs, vice principal at Oak Hill College during my days there, said, 'Liturgy is too important to be left to the liturgists!'

If history judges that *Common Worship* is not a success (and, for all my grumpiness, I hope this will not be the case), then much of the blame must lie with the way that the House of Bishops presently operates.

Meetings of the House of Bishops are pleasant get-togethers of like-minded people and all goes well until they have to get down to business. At that point everyone has to open their briefcases and pull out fistfuls of paperwork. The assumption, of course, is that the bishops will have read and studied their papers beforehand. We had our swots who, infuriatingly, seemed to have read and memorized every paper. One or two bishops always seemed to find a number of amazingly abstruse queries in every document that came before us. They would question the interpretation put on the views of one of the Early Church Fathers on page 41, while their brothers sitting around the tables would raise their eyebrows at each other with knowing smiles.

We would meet at one of three venues, a once-famous hotel in Liverpool that looks like a set from *Titanic*, a modern riverside hotel in York, or a hall in Church House where we all sat behind small tables like schoolboys. I used to enjoy walking up and down the trains to Liverpool or York and counting the number of bishops sitting buried in their papers swotting for the exams ahead.

Each session would be chaired by one of the two archbishops, George Carey or David Hope. They made a superb team, managing to keep us to the tasks without crushing our humanity or those moments when humour breaks through. Speakers and chairmen referred to each other by their dioceses, thus the Archbishop would call on someone to speak by simply saying 'Winchester' or 'Newcastle', and the speaker would refer to others by their full titles – 'The Bishop of Rochester said this, but . . .'. George Carey occasionally tried to encourage the use of Christian names, but it was one area where he was not very successful.

Sitting beside the archbishops would be Philip Mawer, Secretary General to the Synod and a former top civil servant. On more than one occasion, after a prolonged and confusing debate, the chairman would turn to him and say something like, 'And how do you feel we should proceed?' This was really chairman-speak for 'Help!' Without fail, the Secretary General, large notebook in hand, would persuade us that we had seen the issue clearly all along, and that we had three possible courses of action. It was a case of *Yes, Archbishop!*

The agenda paper would have timings set against the many items and there would be provision for times of prayer and reflection. The same paper would also list a string of reports and minutes from working parties and subcommittees of the House. A typical list would have a dozen or so entries, some relating to quite substantial pieces of work, such as the inspection of a theological college. These documents would be sent to the bishops in advance of meetings, and were usually taken as 'deemed business' unless someone asked for a matter to be discussed. Sanity and expedition required such an approach, but it meant that a great deal of hard work was often left undiscussed, and because busy bishops knew in advance that there would be no discussion, those documents may well have been left unread. Occasionally, however, one of the swots would spot a problem in one of these reports, request a time of discussion, and a considerable number of us would be furtively leafing through the pages trying to catch up while the discussion took place.

When it comes to the actual discussion of documents, the usual formula is that someone associated with the working party, or the author of the report, introduces the item and the floor is open for comments and debate. My guess is that many bishops worked as I did. I would study closely those reports where I felt I had some expertise or where I sensed very important issues were at stake. The other reports were skimmed. When a report came to be discussed, therefore, the majority of those present would listen to the minority who knew what they were talking about, and the time would be filled. I learned a great deal from such discussions, but I have to confess that I sometimes woke up to the importance of something halfway through a discussion and kicked myself for not having read that particular paper more closely.

Bishops come in several shapes and quite a number of sizes. There are archbishops, who lead not only their own dioceses but the affairs of a province. In England we have two such provinces, Canterbury and York. There are diocesan bishops, chosen by the Crown Appointments Commission, and the twenty-six most senior of them sit in the House of Lords. There are a few bishops, mostly retired, who are known as assistant bishops, and then there are suffragan bishops, of whom I was one. Suffragans are bishops chosen directly by diocesan bishops to act as their assistants. It has been said that a suffragan bishop is someone who plays second fiddle in a one-man band, but in fact their jobs tend to vary considerably.

Some, indeed, seem to be little more than episcopal curates, while others are assigned to clear-cut areas within their dioceses, acting like mini-diocesans. In Canterbury the Suffragan Bishop of Dover is the virtual diocesan, although he works in partnership with the Bishop of Maidstone across the whole diocese.

Archbishops and diocesan bishops are in the House of Bishops automatically. Suffragan bishops have to stand for election by their peers and some ten places are assigned to those thus elected. I was elected in 1995 to serve for five years. I have to say that I constantly felt there was a slight caste system at work in the House with respect to suffragans. I never really felt that I was a full member of the club, and this probably imaginary feeling was reinforced by occasional comments in debates as to the theological anomalies surrounding suffragan bishops. It is not very reassuring to be a theological anomaly.

What I have to acknowledge, however, is that the bishops with whom I served were a remarkable group of people who would have 'made it to the top' in any profession. I had huge admiration for the ability of many of them to grasp complex issues quickly and talk intelligently about them. The level of theological expertise was high, with only a few of us having to run hard to keep up. Never was this more clearly seen than in the astonishing series of debates we had to conduct concerning a simple two-letter Greek word – ek.

To the outsider it must seem absolutely unbelievable that a two-letter Greek word could cause three lengthy discussions in the House of Bishops and the same number of debates in the General Synod. Some explanation may be enlightening.

We are back again with the compilation of Common Worship, and in particular the creed that was to be used in the

Eucharist. It is known as the 'Nicene Creed' and it supposedly relates back to the Council of Nicaea in AD 325, but the text we call by that name actually relates to a later formulation in 381. When we entered the whole process of liturgical revision, one of the agreed ground rules was that we should use internationally recognized English texts for such items as the Lord's Prayer and the creeds. This meant that we should favourably consider the current texts from the international body known as the English Language Liturgical Consultation (ELLC). The reasoning behind such a position is that we live in an increasingly internationalized world, and it is surely a good thing for English-speaking congregations throughout the world to be using the same texts for these key components of public worship.

The current ELLC text for the Nicene Creed contained the phrase, with regard to the birth of Christ and the 'two natures' reflected within himself: '. . . was incarnate of the Holy Spirit and the Virgin Mary'. When this text was brought before the General Synod for inclusion in the new service, it was met with a negative amendment tabled by none other than my old friend from the 'Hot Pot Coffee School' in Oak Hill, Professor Anthony Thiselton. The professor asked for the text at this point to revert to that which featured in the ASB, namely: 'by the power of the Holy Spirit he became incarnate of the Virgin Mary'.

The General Synod passed Thiselton's amendment and it was sent back to the Liturgical Commission and the House of Bishops. This put the bishops firmly on the spot. Ecclesiastical geopolitics required that they should try to press for the official ELLC text. Practical realities were that the General Synod did not like this text. Many members feared that it did not distinguish between the sort of role played by the Holy Spirit and the sort of role played by Mary in the birth of Christ. There was a strong body of opinion which felt that this elevated Mary improperly. It was also felt that 'of' was too weak a word, lacking the dynamic sense of outgoing movement that many feel is built into the Greek word *ek*.

There were two further problems. First, the ELLC text was a change from both the text used in the ASB and the text used in *The Book of Common Prayer*, which was different yet again ('and was incarnate by the Holy Ghost of the Virgin Mary'). Regular worshippers tended to pick up texts by heart and had liturgical memories. They had just about settled for the ASB after being schooled in the Prayer Book; now there was to be a further version to learn.

The second problem was that scholarship seemed to demand that the ELLC was nearer the mark than either of the other two translations to which English worshippers were accustomed. The oldest Greek texts of the creed only used one preposition to govern both the Holy Spirit's role and Mary's, and that preposition was used only once. The preposition was *ek*. Although Thiselton's amendment and the ASB wanted to perpetuate the long-standing Western or Latin tradition at this point in the creed, the oldest Latin text also used only one preposition for the two. Quite apart from politically correct anxieties about the use of the idea of power on the part of the Holy Spirit, honest scholarship should favour one preposition governing the two.

All this was hammered out in learned ways in the House of Bishops with a strong lead from the Bishop of Ely, formerly Regius Professor of Theology at Cambridge. The bishops decided to stick to their guns, to produce an explanatory report for the members of the Synod and to take the ELLC version back. They argued that *ek* used once was good enough for the original writers of the creed and it should be good enough for us.

But, said some of the more learned members of the General Synod (and there are quite a few of them), is *ek* really best translated as 'of'? Further, Greek prepositions have a greater range of meanings than is the case with our English preposi- tions, thus one can be true to one *ek* and still use the two prep- ositions 'by' and 'of' as was the case in *The Book of Common Prayer*.

By this time the Bishop of Liverpool had broken ranks and pressed for the maintenance of the Prayer Book usage of the two prepositions 'by' and 'of', which he said fitted with litur- gical memory, was true to the spirit of the multi-faceted nature of *ek* and would avoid theological misunderstandings in the pews. After an inconclusive debate, the General Synod sent the matter back to the episcopal drawing board and there was yet another discussion. By then Stephen Sykes had resigned as Bishop of Ely and returned to his first love of uni- versity teaching. Suddenly one discovered that several other bishops, who had kept a low profile in the earlier discussions in the presence of a regius professor, now began to blossom. Yes, said some, perhaps 'of' was too weak a translation of *ek*. There was not enough support for the Bishop of Liverpool's suggestion, but members began to wonder whether some accommodation could be found with Synod's more learned members if we translated *ek* with the English preposition 'from'.

A third debate in the General Synod finally won the day for 'from', but the victory was not overwhelming and there were many, especially in the House of Laity, who felt that some- thing important had been lost.

I found the whole debate fascinating. It revealed that the

House of Bishops contained a considerable number of people of impressive scholarship. It showed them grappling with something more than a two-letter word in another language. They were talking about the age-old mystery of the humanity and divinity of Christ. They were trying to find a way to be true to original intentions dating back to the fourth century, while also trying to be helpful to worshippers and seekers in the twenty-first century. I think we failed, but I am not sure that we would have succeeded with any solution.

My admiration at the abilities of my fellow bishops, however, was continually being blended with a series of uncomfortable questions. As leaders of what the world would call a failing organization, were we performing the right tasks, exhibiting the right gifts, and addressing the right questions? Moreover, did we really have to wade through so much business? Were we leading the Church or merely equipping ourselves to be administrators of a cumbersome regulatory system?

I could not help feeling that we were all working to the wrong job specification and that we had been chosen for the gifts and abilities to carry out the wrong job. As in other levels of the Church's life, we seemed to be dominated by the momentum behind second-order priorities.

For all these uncomfortable feelings about ourselves, there were two occasions when I saw something of the missionary side, and the right qualities coming to the surface. During the first meeting I attended in 1995, after the evening meal on the first day, we were encouraged to brainstorm about the state of the nation and the tasks facing the Church. For ninety stimulating minutes I saw the bishops, liberated from papers, talking about the mission confronting us all. It was a memorable and even exciting session. I was only to see that spirit once more in my five years, and that was when we were encouraged to reflect on the lessons learned from the nation's astonishing response to the death of Diana, Princess of Wales in 1997.

We never debated evangelism save for passing, unenthusiastically, a report about diocesan evangelists and another about establishing a college of evangelists. We never talked about the disturbing church attendance statistics. Instead we were expected to wade through reports on such mouthwatering subjects as 'The Reuilly Common Statement', 'The Cathedrals Measure', 'The Theology of Ordination', 'The Ecclesiastical Jurisdiction (Discipline) Measure', 'Guidelines for the Payment of Parochial and Casual Duty Fees to Retired Clergy', 'Non-stipendiary Ministers and Readers', 'Collegiality in the Service of the *Koinonia* of the Church', 'Amending Canons 22 and 23', 'Review of Synodical Government' . . .

Not everything that came before us was as dry as the list above. Some issues were of importance to both Church and nation. One such was the whole matter of remarriage in church after divorce. This was one of the most difficult issues to come before the House in my time. It was something over which sincere and committed Christians were deeply divided, with both sides making an appeal to the Scriptures. It was something that was a distressing pastoral problem already and to which no solution would be pain- and problem-free. There was, however, another sort of problem with this issue – it was of great interest to the press.

The Church in general and the bishops in particular are not given an easy ride by the press, and this has been the case since the times of Archbishop Ramsey in the later 1960s. If we stick to traditional teachings and practices, we are characterized as being old-fashioned and inflexible. If we encourage any accommodation to present-day culture, we are criticized for being 'trendy'. If bishops speak out, they are often lampooned for being out of touch or dabbling in politics. And if bishops recognize the complexity of some issue and avoid leaping into simplistic comment, they are blamed for not speaking out!

It always seems to me that the media tend to interpret anything that the Church does in the light of well-worn and simplistic stereotypes and themes. Thus bishops are 'woolly' and 'liberal', vicars are 'trendy', numerical decline is related to the abandonment of the Prayer Book and the Authorized Version of the Bible (which does not explain why such decline also affects the Roman Catholics, the Methodists and even the Salvation Army). Any attempt to speak out about social righteousness (a central theme of the Old Testament) is brushed aside as putting politics before spiritual considerations. In this connection it is sobering to note the following words spoken by a well-known politician: 'Churchmen dabbling in politics should note that their only task is to prepare people for the world hereafter.' The politician was Franz Joseph Goebbels, and that fact should be a reminder to all simplistic critics of the Church.

I remember commenting about the sort of treatment that the press accorded to the Church of England in a consultation in London attended by top columnist Melanie Philips. She was asked to comment on my remarks, and startled me by saying:

The media do not like other centres of authority that tell people how to behave. For one thing, they may try to interfere with the media's own agenda! But I would also like to suggest a more controversial reason. The media are not just hostile to the Church because they disapprove of it but because they are in the business of replacing the Church! (cited in *The Quest for Common Values*, Inter Faith Network, 1997, p. 71)

The Church was asking for trouble in producing a report on marriage and divorce which broached the subject of remarriage in church. The subject fell squarely within the stereotype of 'liberal' Church leaders selling the pass on traditional values. It also walked into a more headline-grabbing issue. Was this the Church getting ready to sanction remarriage in church for the Prince of Wales and the divorced woman to which his name was constantly linked?

The exasperating thing for the bishops was that the Church had been agonizing over the issue of remarriage in church since the 1970s, long before Prince Charles married Princess Diana, never mind divorced her. If the bishops deserved criticism, it should have been that for some twenty-five years they had not found a way to regulate a practice that had long been regarded by the General Synod as desirable.

When we came to consider publishing the report on remarriage in church after divorce, much of the discussion centred around the way this might be presented to the public by the press. There were two schools of thought among us. One group felt that we should simply do what was right when it was right, and that we were answerable to God not to the media. There was much talk, at the time, about the use of 'spin doctors' by political parties and we were enjoined not to try to play such a game. The other school of thought, to which I belonged, felt that while we should not try to play spin doctors, we nevertheless needed to weigh up how the press would handle the report and do the best we could to ensure that what we were trying to say was actually heard by the

British public. The troubling reality is that our rank-and-file
members (never mind the wider public) receive most of their
information about the Church of England from the national
media. Relatively few read Church newspapers.

The bishops could see that they were walking a tightrope
on this issue. To permit the remarriage, in church, of
divorced persons (in certain circumstances) could be interpreted as further undermining the importance of marriage
at a time when a third of all marriages were breaking down.
On the other hand, if they did not relax their rules, was this
not a stance that appeared to make marriage breakdown the
only thing in life that was unforgivable? To complicate
matters further, in spite of the Church's official position, a
large number of clergy were already conducting remarriages
in church and had the law of the land on their side in so
doing.

The bishops tried to handle the situation by deciding to
publish a small but excellent document on the importance
of marriage several months before they published the full
report on divorce and remarriage. Their hope was that
people would see that they did indeed want to uphold marriage, and once this point was established the other, more
controversial, report – which was presented as a discussion
document and not an official position – could also be
published.

The end result was neither a victory nor a defeat for our
intentions. The sad thing is that we had to go through all these
contortions simply because we cannot say things directly to
the public, but only through the media, who are not always
concerned to pass on things at face value.

I believe that one of the most disturbing aspects of contemporary society is that the media control so much of the mes-

saging. In a society where community is breaking down and where people live with so little necessary connection to each other, the media have the potential to be uniters. They could be the storytellers that bind people and communities together. Alas, they seem to be more interested in telling the stories that set us against each other.

*   *   *

On a sunny September Sunday in 1997 I was phoned at lunchtime by my elder son. He told me that the *Sunday Times* was running a story that the Prime Minister, Tony Blair, had blocked both the nominations of the Crown Appointments Commission for the new Bishop of Liverpool. The paper was saying that the two men so blocked were 'an archdeacon, and a serving bishop in the southeast of England and a friend of George Carey'. 'Dad,' I was asked, 'could that be you?'

I could only say that as the process for selecting bishops was conducted in strict secrecy, I did not know and could not know.

The next day my secretary came through, ashen-faced, to say that the *Evening Standard* was on the phone and they knew from authoritative sources that the bishop in question was me. It was not long before the *Express* and *The Times* were repeating the story with me firmly in the middle of it. My only response was to say that I seriously doubted whether someone of my age, 63, would have been nominated by the Crown Appointments Commission, and as the whole thing was a secret I was not going to speculate on a speculation.

Up to that point the whole business was a slightly amusing

diversion. Then things began to take a less pleasant turn. The press had sought the views of a number of well-known rent-a-quote clergy, and they were congratulating Tony Blair for refusing to accept the names of yet more of the 'bland characters we've seen in the House of Bishops'. What was needed, we were told, were 'men of vision' – so that put me in my place. Another bemoaned the 'lurch towards the evangelical' and the lack of heavyweights.

By now the press were doing 'research', which meant that they were looking through old cuttings. The *Evening Standard* discovered a garbled report dating back to 1967 when, in a Family Service and to illustrate an important point, I began a sermon by apparently shaving in the pulpit. It lasted thirty seconds, and my talking from the Bible went on for another twelve minutes at least. This discovery was presented to the public as the only thing of significance that I had ever done, and to that was added a sinister note. George Carey and I, it was alleged, were close pals and the Archbishop had been trying to play jobs for the boys. Within a day or so *The Times* was running the same story.

It was then that I began to see the other side of the present, secretive way in which the Church appoints its bishops. Because the name of the game is saying nothing, one not only says nothing to confirm the truth – one also says nothing to contradict what may be false. The silence of an authoritative voice from the Church was being taken as confirmation of the rumour. It was now an unchallenged 'fact' that I was someone not considered good enough by the Prime Minister to be a diocesan bishop. For me, the last straw was when a local paper in Kent reported on a weekend mission I was about to take and stated authoritatively in its second paragraph:

The Bishop of Maidstone was recently in the news when Prime Minister Tony Blair decided not to appoint him as Bishop of Liverpool.

Of course one simply has to get on with things, and there were plenty of things to do. The Liverpool vacancy dragged on and there were spasmodic referrals to my 'rejection' until finally James Jones (who I had always felt was the obvious candidate) was appointed. The truth of the matter was that I felt very angry with a system that was not able or willing to crush the rumour, early on, with a simple denial. It would have spared me a great deal of discouragement. There was also a strange side-effect: I spent so much time saying that I was 'too old to be considered for such a job' that I began to feel I was too old for anything.

When, a few months later, I learned that my colleague the Bishop of Dover was being moved to a key post in Lambeth Palace, I somehow sensed that my own days were numbered.

Mary and I began house-hunting for retirement.

13

Farewell Christian England?

It took me a moment or so to realize what I had just heard the Rabbi say.

I had been meeting, in Church House, Westminster, with a group of leading representatives of the various non-Christian religious communities in England. It was May 1996 and I was talking with them in relation to my work as chairman of the Archbishops' Millennium Advisory Group.

A few months earlier I had met with the then government minister with responsibility for the proposed millennium celebrations. The Conservative government had introduced a national lottery and had been wondering what to do with the profits it hoped to make. By some means or other, it decided to set aside 20 per cent of the proceeds for appropriate ways to celebrate the turn of the century.

I had gone to ask the minister, Mrs Bottomley, how much the government had 'taken on board the fact that the millennium was a Christian festival and had no other rationale outside of the Christian faith'. The date, 2000, or any date for that matter, was meant to be a reminder that we were living in the reign of the King of kings. It was clear that the government had not done much, if any, thinking along such lines, but Mrs Bottomley was a natural enthusiast and a committed Christian, so my words were not falling on hostile ears. She did, however, advance the view that it might prove difficult for Christianity to be placed in the middle of government-sponsored national celebrations as 'that might marginalize the other faith communities'.

I was helped by officials in Church House to identify, through the Inter Faith Network, this group of representatives which met in May. It included two Muslims, two Jews, a distinguished Sikh and a Hindu. I told them what Mrs Bottomley had said about the danger of Christian celebrations in the millennium marginalizing their communities. To my surprise they all smiled and chuckled. The Muslims saw the millennium as a proper opportunity for the largest religious community in the country to put God on the map in a country that was moving towards secularism. The Sikh, Indarjit Singh, saw Jesus as a great religious teacher who ought to be properly commemorated. He even went and said so on two occasions when speaking on the 'Thought for the Day' slot on Radio 4's prestigious *Today* programme. The Rabbi laughed sadly and said, 'We have our festivals – why can't you have yours?'

And then he said it. 'Thank God this is still a Christian country . . .'

As the discussion continued, it became very clear to me that he was not simply quipping. He meant it. I came across the same attitude from another Jew in December 1999. He was an educationalist who worked for an official Jewish organization. We were walking together round the Faith Zone of the Millennium Dome, enjoying a preview two weeks before it was due to open. As we walked round looking at the various contents, I became acutely aware that the whole place was dominated by Christianity. References to the other faith groups in Britain were indeed to be found, but Christianity clearly had pride of place. I was understandably pleased that this was the case, but I could not help wondering what my companion was feeling. Finally I asked him directly, 'Does it not bother you that Christianity gets so much of the space?'

'Oh no,' he said. 'It would have bothered me if Christianity did *not* get most of the space!'

His words and those of the Rabbi at my Church House meeting highlighted one of the things that became clear to me as I continued my involvement in discussions about the millennium. There are very different views in circulation as to the essential character of our national culture. Mrs Bottomley's concern about marginalizing the other faiths only reflected what I continually met from parliamentary figures and those who advised them. We are living, they would claim, in an multi-faith society, and this requires very careful handling if harmony is to exist.

The Churches and their spokespeople sometimes also talk about Britain being a multi-faith society. The words that more often come to the surface, however, are 'increasingly secular', 'plural' and 'post-Christian'. Early in 2002 national newspapers gave prominence to some words of Cardinal Murphy-O'Connor. Speaking to a gathering of Roman Catholic priests, the Cardinal said, 'It does seem . . . especially in England and Wales, that Christianity as a sort of backdrop to people's lives and moral decisions and to the government and to the social life of Britain has now almost been vanquished.'

In fact, the Cardinal was not speaking from a defeatist mind-set, but his words struck a chord with very many who read or heard them. They also appeared to be in sad harmony with some words from an address by Archbishop Carey some months before. The Archbishop – a man whose natural instinct is to be positive and even bullish – was reported as saying, 'A tacit atheism prevails. Death is assumed to be the end of life. Our concentration on the here-and-now renders the thought of eternity irrelevant.'

It is understandable to use language similar to these words quoted from the two leaders of England's largest Churches. This book started by describing the England of the 1930s when I was baptized and the England of the 1940s when I attended Sunday school, as did the majority of British children. Such days are certainly behind us. Much smaller numbers of children are presented for baptism, and alas not all of them seem to be made welcome. Nowhere near a majority of the nation's children are to be found in our Sunday schools; indeed, the institution itself appears to be on its last legs. It is fair to say that Christianity does not come readily to people's minds as a familiar component of national life. Anna Blundy, writing in *The Times* magazine on the 16th March 2002, claimed to see a renewal of interest in churchgoing on the part of young professionals with children. She suggested that there were a number of reasons for this phenomenon, including gaining eligibility for their children to go to Church schools. She contrasted this apparently promising sign with 'Christianity's strange stigma' in the very society in which these young professionals move. One person she interviewed said:

It is embarrassing. It just doesn't have the exotic multiculturalism of saying 'I go to the synagogue' or 'I go to the mosque'. I met a woman in the doctor's the other day and was explaining to the receptionist that we knew each other from church. I could actually see the receptionist freeze up in horror.

Blundy went on to conclude: 'It is true that going to church seems to be something to keep quiet about.' How then are we to describe the culture of this country? Is it now multi-faith? Is it post-Christian and increasingly secular? Or could it be that the Rabbi was speaking a true word in the midst of his jest?

Of one thing I am clear. This is not a multi-faith society if by that we mean that there are a number of similarly sized and competing religious communities. It is quite true that today's Britain includes Hindus, Sikhs, Muslims and Buddhists, and that it has long had a remarkable Jewish community. We need to be clear, however, that with the exception of a relatively small number of areas, such faith communities have not placed their stamp on the culture. It is true that we can all think of towns and cities and suburbs where people of Asian origin have settled in numbers, and mosques and temples are to be found. There are often totally Asian neighbourhoods. If, however, one was to prepare a colour-coded map of Britain's religious communities, the colour for Christianity (albeit nominal) would swamp all other colours. When all the religious communities apart from Christianity are added together, we are still looking at significantly less than 10 per cent of the population.

Obviously there is a danger in saying this. It could be seen as implying that minority groups are somehow inferior and can be ignored. That must never be allowed to happen. The fact remains, however, that the fortunes of England and Christianity have been entwined since Augustine came to Canterbury, indeed even before. To talk as if other faiths were of equal cultural significance is simply to refuse to face facts and to do harm to the nation's sense of identity. It may be politically correct to lump all the faith communities together in the well-intentioned hope of affirming all, but it is unwise when the vast majority of the population claim some nominal link to Christianity.

In a lecture given in Durham in 2001, Roy Strong, former director of the Victoria and Albert Museum, spoke critically about 'the excesses of political correctness and the cult of subservience to minorities'. When I spoke to that meeting in Church House, I found that the Muslims wanted the Christian Churches, because of their greater strength, to lead the battle against encroaching secularism. They did not want their existence to be an excuse for a politically correct downplaying of the Christian significance of the millennium.

It is not an argument against describing England as 'Christian' to point to the existence of other faiths. One has to examine the numerical strength of the other faith groups, and one has to ask whether the everyday feel of life carries a strong imprint from one or all of these other faiths.

It has become increasingly common in recent years to stress that Christianity is in decline and is itself only a minority group. There are two responses to these charges. The first is to admit that church attendance statistics across all the major denominations have shown steady falls over the last thirty or forty years. Only the Baptists appear to be bucking this trend. One of the mitigating factors that needs to be set against these figures, however, is that of the overall decline in all forms of public association in Western European countries. For forty years there has been a steady decline in people joining groups, clubs and movements, and attending public entertainments. Television and the private car have played a big part in this. Some, but not all, of the decline in church attendance can be set against these overall trends. More recent times have seen the development of the consumer mind-set which encourages people to see life as a range of options from which one picks and chooses according to felt needs at the time. This again militates against 'joining' and commitments.

The second response is to acknowledge that the Christian Churches are a minority group within the total population, but to ask where and what the majority group may be. The logic of saying that Christianity is a minority group is the implication that somehow a majority group exists which keeps Christianity firmly in its shadow. The fact is that there is no such majority group. Contemporary Britain is a nation of minority groups. When looked at in this light the Christian denominations, when added together, make up the largest of these minority groups by far. Many more people are united in common cause because of Christianity than are to be found united in support of any other cause or worldview. You do not need to have over 50 per cent of the population to be the most significant element in that population.

My conclusion is that Britain is not multi-faith in its cultural character, but I believe that a growing relationship of trust and common cause between the various religious communities is essential for a healthy future.

By the same token, I do not believe that Britain is a secular country. The largest identifiable groupings in the country are marked by religious faith. The events to which the nation turns in times of crisis and disaster are, as often as not, televised religious gatherings in the great cathedrals. The tragic death of Diana, Princess of Wales in 1997 did not unleash a massive demonstration of secular angst. It released an astonishing response characterized by the use of flowers to create sacred spaces and by a massive resort to places of worship. The Churches were caught off balance by what happened, but they were still able to act as the conduits for grief.

The process of secularization has, indeed, been taking place in our country, at least since the Second World War. Areas of activity that were once the preserve of the Churches, or voluntary groups often dominated by Christians, have been taken over by national and local government agencies. The welfare state replaced a great deal of charitable Christian effort. Two things need to be said. First, it can be argued that the welfare state is actually evidence of the place of Christianity within the culture. The idea of loving one's neighbour did not first appear in a government white paper! Second, in both America and Britain we may be seeing the beginnings of desecularization, with governments wanting to turn areas of social concern back to the Churches and the other faith communities. The logical demands of low-tax economies are that voluntary agencies become increasingly important as providers of social welfare. The realities of voluntary agencies are that they are often specifically Christian and that many who volunteer do so from Christian motivations.

If, therefore, England is not multi-faith and not secular, how can it be described? My answer, strongly reinforced by my experiences as a bishop, is that the Rabbi was right: 'This is still a Christian country.'

To quote Roy Strong again:

In spite of all our multifaith and multicultural society, the truth of the matter is that Britain is still overwhelmingly a Christian country . . . No amount of relabelling Christmas Luminos or Winterval is going to eradicate our two millennia as a Christian nation.

I have come to agree with his conclusion, while sitting loose to his mathematics! As he and others like him would point out, you cannot make much sense of the country's built heritage, its art and literature, much of its law, its moral attitudes and its public institutions without recognizing the direct inspiration of Christianity.

That said, I would acknowledge that this cultural Christianity is in a state of lapse. In a cultural sense we are losing our memory, but the memory we are losing is a memory of the story of Christ. For many years Christianity has been increasingly less obvious as a guide and inspiration to our society, but there is no evidence that it is being replaced by any rival coherent philosophy of life, unless materialism, consumerism and an ill-considered pluralism be granted such status. The much-discussed 'postmodern' mind-set is one that questions the possibility of any clear-cut values and meanings to life.

I believe it is important that Christians start saying this louder and more often. The people who want Christianity to fade away quietly are not our friends in the other faiths, but those who carry secularizing agendas. They are to be found in strength in the worlds of media and politics. They need to be challenged, and in particular their frequent references to the numerical weaknesses of the Churches need to be countered. While truth cannot be measured by popularity, it remains important to point out that the Churches are far stronger numerically than is often reported. Some of this understating has been assisted by the Church of England's past approach to statistics. In 2002 new figures were released by the Church based on more appropriate ways of counting. They revealed that Christmas attendances in 2000 were just under 3 million people, whereas previous calculations had been based on the numbers receiving Communion, which was only about half that number. Again previous reports of usual Sunday attendances (USAs) had put the attendance levels nationally at around 0.97 million, whereas a method of counting using the week, rather than Sunday, as the basic theatre of attendance suggested that we should be looking at about 1.3 million.

These figures only represent the Anglican proportion of national attendances. They need to be multiplied by a factor of three to get an approximate overall figure. The new Church Life Profile studying congregational life in England, presenting its interim report in 2001, concluded, 'For every five people who attend church weekly, there are another three or four who attend at least monthly.' It suggested that one needs to multiply the usual Sunday attendance by three to get a more accurate estimate of the number of English people who worship on a regular or occasional basis. The truth is that about 20 per cent of the population attend public worship with some degree of regularity, and another 40 per cent of the population would claim to have some sort of belief in the Christian tradition.

With these things in mind, it does not make sense for Christians to give up on the concept of Christian England and for us to talk pessimistically about future prospects. On the other hand, there is no cause for complacency.

I remember seeing a film which purported to tell a true story dating back to the Second World War. It concerned the crew of a tanker trying to get much-needed fuel to Malta which was under continuous attack. The ship, the *San Demetrio*, was badly hit by enemy bombers in the Mediterranean. It caught fire and developed a list. The crew took to the boats, sensing that the ship was doomed. They floated around waiting for help for a day or so until they caught sight of a ship on the horizon. They rowed towards it, only to find that it was their very own *San Demetrio*! It had not sunk. They decided to reboard the ship, battle with its fires and try to get it sailing again. To cut a moving story short, they succeeded. That story spoke to me about people who abandoned ship too soon, and it also spoke to me of the crew discovering that the ship was still there and that, in their absence, no one else had taken over.

That is my picture of Christian England. I believe that the Churches have, to a large extent, abandoned the ship too soon, and that no one else has effectively taken over. I believe that it is time to get back on board to see if we can make things work again. The great task before all the Churches – and it needs *all* the Churches – is the re-establishment of Christianity within the life and culture of our society.

Not all Christians, however, warm to such an idea. There are those who feel that 'Christian England' talk is about the encouragement of semi-commitment, and who feel that the present 'post-Christian' or 'increasingly secular' understanding of the situation liberates the Church to be prophetic and evangelistic. There are others who feel that the old 'Christian England' was really about privilege and power and that, rightfully, we have moved on. I do not believe that the essence of Christian England in the past was anything to do with privilege or the encouragement of nominal beliefs. It was certainly nothing to do with bishops in the House of Lords. It was, and it should always be, about the widespread knowledge of the story of Jesus. For me, a Christian society is one where the story is universally known, where Christ himself is admired at least as an example, and where his life and teachings are seen as the yardstick for the nation's core values.

As I have said, the story can be seen as the gold standard underpinning our moral currency. It inspires a concern for fair play and justice. It calls for the protection of the weak. It sets people the goals of loving their neighbour and practising forgiveness. It motivates people to consider self-sacrifice and service in a selfish world. It recognizes that the way of gentleness achieves more than the path of power. It hints that all of us may well be held accountable for our lives. All those values are essentially Christian and can be directly related to the one story of the one person. The fact that these values make common cause with the teachings of several other faiths is a bonus, but it is not something that should make us soft-pedal the story. Those story-values can be actively pursued by those who cannot bring themselves to believe in the divinity of Christ, but such a pursuit depends on the cultural memory remaining fresh.

In a strange way, an over-emphasis on evangelizing people can make evangelizing people more difficult. We need to evangelize the culture just as much. We need to keep the memory of Christ strong in the corporate mind. Doing that is right in itself and has the side-effect of creating fertile soil for the sowing of the gospel in people's lives. If people grow up in a state of unfamiliarity with the story of Christ, then Christians have fewer starting points for the sharing of their faith.

If we are to strengthen the memory of Christ in our society, where do we begin? *We begin with children*. The old Sunday school was probably the biggest factor in the creation and maintenance of a country that remembered the story of Jesus. It is hard to be exact about the percentage of children who went through Sunday school in the early decades of the twentieth century, but we are certainly talking about over half the population. One of the remarkable things about the old Sunday school was that it bridged the social classes. Many working-class adults felt that church was for the middle classes and that they did not fit, but they still sent their children to learn the old, old story. Those children grew up to be like their parents: non-attenders, but non-attenders who knew the story. This is decreasingly so with respect to present-day non-attenders. Sunday school created fringes for the congregations, and people open to pastoral contacts. Increasingly today there is a polarization between those who are insiders and those who are outsiders. It may please tidy minds, but I doubt whether it reflects the mind of the Christ who offered friendship to all.

As I have said earlier, however, a return to the old Sunday school is a highly unlikely prospect. We have to work with the rub of society as it now is, but we have the real advantage that children are accessible and clubbable. Wherever churches or Christian groups have thought imaginatively about times, venues and formats, children have been reached and often in large numbers. They will not come to school-type settings, but they will come to events where there will be fun, activity and music, and they will listen to stories and they will ask astonishingly profound questions. If they have enjoyed themselves, and if they have admired those who told them of Christ, they will remember for the rest of their lives.

The problem the Churches face is not whether they can reach children, but whether they want to do it and whether they are prepared and able to invest the energy. It is here that we run into two unhelpful realities of church life today. First, many church members are elderly with limited energies; and second, many younger church members work long hours and are often over-committed in church affairs during their free time. If a massive move into children's ministry is to take place, then – locally and nationally – priorities will have to change. Too many churches are entertaining their members when they should be putting them to work.

I am convinced that the Churches could reach over a

quarter and possibly over a third of today's children if they really wanted to do it. Were that to happen, several things would follow. First, there would be stronger, and more specifically Christian, youth work in our churches within ten years. Second, there would be more young adults in our congregations in fifteen to twenty years. Third, there would be more younger candidates for ordained ministry. Fourth, the Christian 'feel' to our society would increase rather than decrease.

The second emphasis in a strategy to re-establish the place of Christianity must be an emphasis on community building on the part of the Churches. It has become fashionable to lament the fact that churches carry smaller fringes than once was the case, and indeed it is something I often used to say. Part of this shrinkage relates to the weakening of children's work over a long period of time. I have come to believe, however, that part of the problem relates to deliberate choices made by congregations and Christian ministers. The fact of the matter is that fringes can still be built. The price, however, is congregations with messy edges to the outside world.

Increasingly, over the last thirty years, I have seen congregations developing insider mentalities, often claiming that this is the consequence of 'renewal'. Many clergy have increasingly busied themselves in arranging the affairs of those who already come. I can remember the parish representatives of a church that was seeking a new incumbent expressing surprise that one applicant for the vacant post of vicar wanted to spend time in the schools of the parish. They actually asked, 'What does he want to do that for?' Not surprisingly, the congregation only numbered about twenty-five in a parish of over 15,000 people. I believe good relationships with schools are vital to the creation of community.

One of the subtle changes in the Church of England over my time as a minister has been a shift from seeing the community as the main field of concern, to seeing the congregation as the centre of attention. In many places the church noticeboard ought to be headed 'Anglican Congregational Church' rather than 'Church of England'. Twenty-five years of talk about 'church growth' has left me wondering whether this has been at the expense of 'kingdom widening'. A fashionable term in recent years has been 'finding new ways of being church'. I have a great deal of sympathy for this agenda, but I also feel we need more talk of 'new ways of being un-church'!

Of course, community building is a complex matter. In rural areas it is usually a mistake for the church to try to build an inward-looking community around itself. The community is already there and waiting for the church to play its part within what already exists. In suburbia, in featureless estates and in the inner city one often finds that there is little or no sense of community and that people find community through their own networks. That is where churches, with patience, can often create an attracting and serving community.

In the Canterbury diocese I found that those churches which tried to build bridges into the wider community were usually the churches that had fringes and which grew numerically. I also saw that where the parish priest saw him or herself as a sort of chaplain to the area, as well as the leader of the congregation, that ministry was appreciated. There would be goodwill towards the church and this would show in terms of attendances at times such as Christmas, Harvest Festival, Mothering Sunday and Remembrance Sunday. I also found that those churches that tried to market their services on those big Sundays in the year usually saw the benefit of their effort and imagination.

The typical range of activities in community-building churches also included good relationships with schools (county schools as well as Church schools), playgroups and parents and toddlers groups, weekday children's activities, and social activities and services appropriate to the needs of the area.

The best way to create community is to serve community, and I believe that with the first evidences of a drift towards desecularizing social concern, the churches face a challenging and fruitful future as servant communities to those around them.

A third plank in a strategy for re-establishing Christianity in the country has to be improving the attractiveness of our public worship. The more we hold on to our congregations and the more we add, the stronger will be the Christian contribution to the community at large. When the memory of Christ pervades a society, the conditions are in place for nominal believers and seekers to consider 'going to church'. This is why we need to offer services which start where such people find themselves, and this is why the exclusion of model Family Services in *Common Worship* has been so short-sighted.

As long ago as 1945 and *Towards the Conversion of England*, parish churches were encouraged to see public worship as, itself, a bridging activity that could draw people in. The report called for flexibility and imagination. This brings into question not only strict adherence to official worship forms, but also the growing practice of majoring on the Eucharist as the main, and sometimes the only, service on offer. As I said earlier, there is a clear mismatch between what seekers need and what we are offering. That may be acceptable in a gathered church, but it is not acceptable in a Church claiming to be the inclusive Church that serves England.

We need more informal services, but that does not mean that the statutory forms of service have to be written off in terms of their drawing potential. My colleague in my latter years in Canterbury, Bishop Stephen Venner, used to find that clergy and readers often put a great deal of imagination and creative energy into Family Services, but considerably less into the statutory services of the Prayer Book and the ASB (as it then was). Usually he would be told that the Family Services drew higher attendances. His challenge to the parishes was that if they put as much imagination into how they presented their ASB and Prayer Book services, they might see more people coming to them as well.

The day is long past when we can rely on congregations coming out of a sense of obligation. In our consumer age, most people will only come when they are sure that they will be presented with something worthwhile. Churches have got to see their public services as their shop windows. Never is this more so than in the major festivals and folk religion moments mentioned earlier, namely Christmas, Mothering Sunday, Harvest Festival and Remembrance Sunday and, to a lesser extent, Easter. These are times when the churches are presented with tremendous opportunities to reinforce and widen the public memory of Christ, and they must be seized.

A fourth plank in a strategy to re-establish Christianity within the culture is the encouragement of creativity and artistic flair within our congregations. We need new Christian authors, artists and musicians to make their contributions into the evolving culture of our society. The pen and the brush are often more powerful than the sword and the businessman's chequebook. This is a little understood area and it is to the credit of the Roman Catholic Church that it seems to be more successful than other traditions. This is not unrelated to the place of colour and drama in its liturgical life, but it is also something to do with the fact that evangelicals too often want their artists to be propagandists.

While all these things are happening, I can see that our Church leaders will need to engage in a number of dialogues with the media and the political parties. We have got to convince people that the healthier the churches, the more the likelihood of increasing voluntary service. We have got to convince the opinion-formers that the story of Jesus enhances community life and not the reverse. There are a number of half-truths that need to be challenged. The first of these is that religions are inevitably sources of conflict. Places like Northern Ireland and the Middle East are often cited in support of such a perception. We have got to be able to point to the many places and situations where Christianity has inspired unselfish service.

As the twenty-first century opened, a debate was raging over the place of 'faith-based schools'. It was government policy to put money into the foundation of a number of new 'faith-based schools' (which is the politically correct way of saying 'Church schools' in most cases). It has become fashionable to claim that an increase of Church schools would be divisive in our multi-faith society. I have already queried the accuracy of this perception of Britain as a multi-faith society. I would also want to query this strange notion that a Church school creates bigots. The truth, in England at least, is quite the opposite. I fail to see how a school that seeks to work out of an ethos that reflects Christian values can easily turn out bigots. The Christ we acknowledge told us to love our enemies, to forgive those who despitefully use us, and to follow his example in these and other matters. We need more people schooled in these values if our society is to flourish. They are the values of social coherence rather than fragmentation.

There is also a need to challenge the ill-considered logic of so-called 'inclusivism'. At first glance it is surely a virtuous aspiration for a modern nation. A second glance reveals, however, that the perceived wisdom about creating an inclusive society is to press the faith communities to keep quiet about their distinctive positions. Distinctive views are seen to be hostile to the vision of a harmonious multi-faith and multi-cultural society. What the leaders of the various faiths would want to say in reply is that integrity is important to them and that public witness to their distinctives is the requirement of integrity. What is possible, however, is a respect for each other's distinctive beliefs and thereby a respect for each other's integrity. A society cannot call itself 'free' if there cannot be the open exchange of differing views and opinions.

*　*　*

One of the lessons to be learned from the Decade of Evangelism is that the missionary task goes far deeper than simply finding some new and more effective technique for 'bringing people to Christ'. George Lings, the imaginative and well-informed church-planting and evangelistic guru of the Church Army, once said in my hearing that evangelism had many similarities to agriculture.

He spoke about an over-emphasis on reaping machinery when what was probably needed was more attention to sowing the seed. He did not leave it there, however. He went on to say that no effective farmer thought about sowing without also paying attention to the state of the soil.

The culture of a community is all about the soil in which its members are planted and either flourish or wither. I think the biggest lesson of the Decade has been that we have paid too little attention to the state of the soil. I also think that it is not too late to start doing that thinking. Christian England may well be recoverable. It will not be the same as earlier versions, but that is probably a good thing. A society inspired by the story of Jesus, which is not the same thing as a society where everyone is a Christian, is worth working for. May the cause fare well.

14

A Church for the People

Everyone, especially the children, knew her as Aunt Sally. Her real name was Mrs Marshall and she was the wife of the local doctor. I met her when, during the unsettled years of the war, I went to live with relatives in the rural outskirts of Sheffield. I was about eight years old and friendless. My uncle and aunt decided that I needed to be introduced to Aunt Sally.

Aunt Sally had become the Pied Piper for the children of that area. It had all started, I was told, when she was helping her sickly elder son to recover from a serious illness and find his feet with other children. The third-floor nursery became a buzzing centre of activity, with frequent rushes to the window to see express trains racing through nearby Dore and Totley Station on their way to Sheffield. I soon learned the importance of collecting train numbers.

Aunt Sally taught me to ride a bike, play tin-can hockey and improve my cricket. By this time her elder son was truly mended, away at public school and well on his way to becoming a Scottish rugby international. One thing I kept noticing, as I spent so much time at her house, was her disappearance practically every morning. She never said where she was going, but she would jump on her bicycle and pedal away for about half an hour.

One day, when I was not at Aunt Sally's house, I was walking past the local parish church when I spotted her bike leaning against the church wall. Being a nosey youngster, I crept to the door and looked in, and the daily mystery of Aunt Sally's disappearance was answered. There she was, kneeling in her church, catching some respite from the bustle of the nursery, and saying her prayers.

Why do I tell this story? It will become apparent.

Anne Quilliam was the parish worker at St Philemon's, Toxteth, in the 1970s when I spent several days in the parish. I had been asked by her colleague, Colin Bedford, to visit, appraise and think out a possible mission to the parish. As part of the visit I was meeting some key people, and this is where Anne came in. 'You must meet "Lal" Lomas,' she said.

I was taken to a small terraced house, where Lal came to the door to welcome us into her home. She was frail and elderly, but one quickly sensed that she was more than a little 'special'. I shall never forget Anne's first words to her on that cold winter day. 'Where are you today, Lal?' she asked. I was more than a little surprised at Anne's words, but even more so at Lal's answer. 'South America,' she said.

While I was wondering whether Anne was humouring someone who was a little odd, I was shown into the kitchen and saw what the conversation was all about. There on the table was a spread of prayer literature for mission agencies working in South America. I was in the presence of someone who had a tremendous ministry of intercession. I learned that Lal set apart sessions every day of the week when she would concentrate on praying for God's work in some part of the world, not forgetting Toxteth.

Why have I told this story? It will become apparent.

The scene moves back to my curacy days in East Ham. I have already mentioned the large and lively youth fellowship. Most of the young people were extremely able. They would enjoy taking part in Bible studies and discussion groups as much as they enjoyed boisterous games and parish parties. I remember one lad, however, who was a bit different. I shall call him Donald. He was shy and tended to keep in the background, watching the extroverts with admiration. He was no great talker or sharer of profound thoughts. Discussing the Bible was not quite his scene.

In the freezing winter of 1962/3, however, Donald came into his own. When it had become clear that we were facing a prolonged cold spell, I thought it would be good to ask the youth fellowship members to adopt elderly people and visit regularly to see how they were coping. They were soon tackling the task with more discipline than I expected. In most cases the elderly people were coping well, and it was our youngsters who came away filled with warming cups of tea and good east London conversation. Donald, however, found that his elderly couple, in a flat up several flights of stairs, were in trouble.

They had run out of coal and they were freezing. I do not know how Donald did it. I think he pleaded hard-luck stories to everyone he met. Whatever his strategy, the end result was that he dashed up the stairs, day after day, carrying buckets of coal – until the thaw came and financial help with it for his old people. As I watched what Donald was doing, I realized that at last Christianity was becoming real to him. This was something he could do for God, and he made sure it was done.

Why do I tell this story? It will become apparent.

Robin Murch, a former army officer and struggling with deafness, had been beavering away as Vicar of Queensborough on the Isle of Sheppey for many years before I arrived to be his bishop. He was not one of the world's greatest preachers and his congregation was a small one, meeting in an ancient building in the middle of an area that had known better days.

I remember making a parish visit to Queensborough and talking through his ministry and the ministry of his congregation. 'Tell me,' I asked, 'are there any needs out there in the community that the church is trying to address?' It was one of the questions we were asking on all the parish visits that year. Robin looked at me with a quiet smile. 'Bishop,' he said, 'we in the congregation are the casualties. We don't have to go outside the congregation to find great areas of need.' He was right, but I also knew that he went outside his congregation with care and concern a great deal.

I visited a nearby school and spoke with the head teacher, who claimed to be an atheist. He looked across at Robin and said to me quietly, 'The man's a saint. Everybody loves him!'

The day came when the Archbishop put his staff on notice to discuss the filling of a number of vacant honorary canonries in the cathedral. People who are made canons are usually the high-fliers in the diocese. Canonries are a sort of honours list in the Church. Patrick Evans, Robin's archdeacon, and I made up our minds to suggest Robin's name.

As the discussion flowed in the staff meeting, various skilled and talented clergy were named. Then it came to Patrick and myself. 'We would like to suggest Robin Murch,' we said, wondering what chance he would have against the other prestigious names before us.

There was a moment of unusual silence. I looked up to see

that everyone round the table was smiling, and then the same word came from just about every mouth: 'Yes!'

Why do I tell this story? It will become apparent.

At the sports centre in Ashford a performance of *Scrooge* was being presented by youngsters, mainly from the sprawling new estates around the nearby small village of Kingsnorth where Sheila McLachlin worked as vicar. Sheila started with very little on the ground by way of children's or youth work. The church council had to be persuaded to 'risk' having a woman vicar in the first place. It was not long before they realized they had landed a gem of a person.

Helped by a small but talented group of parishioners, Sheila somehow hit on the idea that, while coming to church was no big deal for the many youngsters moving into the area, joining a drama group committed to mounting a show certainly had an appeal. They decided to do *Scrooge* because it was fun and because it carried a message not far from the heart of Christianity. At least fifty young people became involved. As they rehearsed, they were only too ready to be led in prayer for the success of the project.

I was asked to attend the performance, and Sheila is one of those people whose invitations are like three-line whips. Mary and I both went, as did the local member of parliament. The show was full of fun and vivacity. Yes, there were moments when things went wrong and beards came unstuck, but the whole thing was a triumph. The youngsters were made to feel that they mattered, and the vision of a parish priest was vindicated. And what about the bishop in the front row? He just sat there at the end, clapping until his hands hurt and blinking through his tears.

Why do I tell this story? I tell it, as I have told the earlier stories, and could tell more, because they all have one thing in common. They are about the reality of the Church of England. They are about ordinary people trying to serve God and those around them, all linked together in the strange enterprise known as the Church of England. I have mentioned others earlier in the book: Miss Seeley, Mr Dick, the stately Miss Barton with her tea party, Charlie Cope giving his every spare moment to helping youngsters like me discover Christ. I have talked about the east London dockers and Ford workers who put church before the pub, who liked a good laugh and a good sermon, and who were well served by a fun-loving vicar. I have mentioned the faithful work of my colleagues in CPAS, and the clergy and people of Canterbury diocese who kept their heads down and kept going even when there was little to show for their labours. I could have listed hundreds – no, thousands – of sincere people, clerical and lay, whom I have seen and known over the years, all of us keeping company in and with our funny old Church.

And I tell these stories because I am saddened by those who type out shallow mockeries for their press columns, telling us of emptying pews, trendy vicars and weak bishops, distorting the true import of General Synod debates and reports, and picking up their pay cheques in the reassuring knowledge that the Church does not sue. We are rarely told about the ordinary people, thousands and thousands of them, who in pulpit, pew or community simply do their best for God.

The media feed on describing crises, and the Church of England seems to have plenty to describe. To the media, however, a crisis is about failure and people getting things wrong, and hopefully about blame. To a Christian with a strong belief in providence, a crisis is something that God allows and through which he presents a challenge to the faithful. When I retired I left behind a diocese which, like other dioceses, was facing the challenges of several interlocking crises. What follows are the sorts of thoughts which I was having in my final months as a serving bishop and which have continued with me since. I do not share them as some sort of blueprint for putting things right. I am not that sure of my ground. I share them because they reveal the types of issues that are engaging many in the Church of England as we enter the twenty-first century.

One of the things that was becoming clear to me in my final months was that churches have energy levels. For a congregation, energy is measured in terms of available human effort, and money. Because of the chronic weakness in reaching and holding children, young people and young families in recent years, our congregations are increasingly elderly. That means that human energy levels are more limited and it also means that money is equally limited because of the number of people on pensions and fixed incomes.

If we ask a church to live beyond its energy levels it will soon be in trouble, and this is beginning to happen. I think of two parochial church councils that I met in the course of my round of parish visits. The first concerns a PCC where discussion revealed that their congregation of sixty to seventy had to find £600 every week to pay the quota. Admittedly, two thirds of that sum was the cost of the pay, pension and housing of their parish priest, but it was still a large sum to find. It meant that before they could spend money on the repairs to their historic building, or pay the working expenses of their clergy, or buy equipment for their children's work, or pay their heating bills, £600 had to be found and paid into central diocesan funds.

Leaving aside the cost of providing central services in each diocese, about £17 million is needed from the parishes to finance the central services of the national Church each year, more than half of which goes on the training of clergy and other ministerial concerns. That averages out at just over £1,300 per parish, and as very many of our parishes are tiny the sum to average-sized congregations is much more. All this is a drain on local church energy, and although it is right to expect congregations to pay a price for being part of a larger Church and a larger cause, it is also right to ask whether we are asking too big a price. We also need to remember that individual members and congregations are also giving to support national and international Christian work and other charitable causes.

The second church council meeting that comes to mind took place in a historic Norman church which was continuously needing repair and renovation. In the few years before I sat down to talk with the council they had raised over £200,000 for work on the building. Every time some work could be funded and was put in hand, further expensive problems would reveal themselves. It was like throwing money into a black hole. As we talked about these problems, one council member said to me, 'Bishop, we just want out. We've had enough.' They wanted to be able to worship in the warmth, and to have the energy to reach out to the parish with the gospel rather than a begging bowl.

Every year the Church of England has to find around £100 million for the maintenance of its stock of historic buildings. Church buildings form a massive proportion of England's built heritage, and people are quick to lament if our buildings are in poor repair, but precious little help comes from the government. Indeed, a large part of the repair bills paid by the Church goes to the government in terms of value added tax on work completed. I have a feeling that the next big crisis facing the Church of England will be a rebellion by congregations against the burden of historic buildings.

There are other energy-consuming aspects. Our legal organizational procedures for parishes are a burden on the smaller parishes and multi-parish benefices. Our synodical system, local and national, brings busy church members together to discuss reports and contract business, much of which has little bearing on the week-by-week life of the churches.

If the English denominations were horses in a handicap race, the Church of England would be top weight by a very large amount. For some time I have been interested to find the reason why the Baptist Union is the only major denomination in England that is not in steady decline. I think one of the reasons is that it travels very light, treasuring the independency of its congregations and keeping its central structures commendably compact.

This prompts me to say that the leadership of the Church of England needs the courage to downsize. We do not like to talk in these terms. We see them as defeatist and admissions of failure. Every gardener, however, knows that pruning is all about encouraging new life through ensuring that energy levels are concentrated in the right places. It is a bad gardener who refuses to prune.

In fact, the Church has been downsizing for the last twenty-five years at least. Much of this, however, has been on an *ad hoc* basis, and much of the pain has been borne by the parishes. Central slimming has not been proportionate to cutbacks in the deaneries. Parishes have been amalgamated so that we can operate with the ever-decreasing numbers of clergy. So often these amalgamations have been made when a

priest retires or moves. This has meant that a parish is joined
to another simply because it is vacant and not as part of a
carefully thought out strategy. In my final year or so in
Canterbury diocese we were trying to get deaneries to look
ahead and make plans for the future over a five- to ten-year
scenario, so that we could identify what would be the best
deployment of fewer stipendiary clergy well in advance of
having to make the decisions. The dominating concern was
not that of ensuring survival, but of giving ourselves a chance
of growth.

What we saw to be important was that while stipendiary
clergy were vital, they should not become the only consideration in the future of churches. Some parishes could go forward
with lay leadership or non-stipendiary clergy. The Church of
England is nothing if it is not a church for the people. It
cannot be driven by a policy that is dominated by the number
of available stipendiary clergy. We need to develop a new way
of thinking about ministry. We need a 'do-it-yourself' lay
culture to replace the over-clericalistic one of past decades.
Changes in the right direction have been taking place for
thirty years or so, but we are still too timid.

In 1999 our Diocesan Synod in Canterbury passed a resolution that was meant to go up the line to General Synod. Its
thrust was simple. We said that the time had come for the
centre to stop increasing financial demands on the dioceses
and parishes. If the Church of England is essentially to be a
church for the people of the country, then it must be organized
so that its work among people, such as the congregations and
chaplaincies, is seen as the top priority area, not its central
structures. It is in the congregations, through the witness in
daily life of their members, and through those Christian
workers serving hospitals, prisons, colleges and distinct

people groups, that the gospel is shared and the kingdom extended. To weaken those key areas of mission in order to fund central operations is not an acceptable way forward. To put things bluntly, the General Synod and the new Archbishops' Council may have important jobs to do, but they put down no rubber on the real roads of engagement with society.

I believe that we have to slim down our central structures radically, both nationally and in the dioceses. They are all relatively young in Church history terms, so they cannot be regarded as essential to the life of the Church. They exist, in the main, as servant structures. If it can be shown that they are hampering the flourishing of congregational life, we must rethink. I am reluctantly coming to the view that the General Synod in its present form, and its related boards, may have to be seriously cut back. I am sure we need some sort of synodical forum bringing bishops, clergy and laity together in decision-making, but synods are like motorways. If you open a new motorway you will actually increase the amount of traffic. If you hold two or three General Synod meetings a year, you will – by some mysterious principle – produce enough business to justify the meetings. I think we should limit the General Synod to one meeting a year and if that means that we can contract less business, then the chances are that we will learn to prioritize better.

My experience of working on a General Synod report has left me feeling very sceptical of their value. Over the years I have, far too often, seen reports commissioned, produced, sent round the dioceses and debated in General Synod, only to end up forgotten or ignored. In practically every case, the reports are published by the Church's publishing arm, and hundreds of free copies are sent out to Synod members. The amount of time and money expended must be prodigious, but apart from *Faith in the City* I can think of very few reports which have made any real difference to anything. Indeed, at times reports can prove damaging to the Church. Because they are commissioned by the Church, and because they are published by the official Church publishing department, the media tend to regard them as the 'official positions' of the Church when most are actually awaiting formal debates in Synod.

In 1995 a report on family life was produced for the General Synod under the title of *Something to Celebrate*. Its style was not so much to prescribe ideal ways forward as to describe the full range of relationships that were now to be found in our society. While there was some theological reflection on what was being described, the whole approach contained hostages to fortune in terms of how the press might present it to the general public. When the debate on the report actually took place, the report itself had been published for several weeks and was not only being presented in distorted terms by the British media but, as I found in Argentina, throughout the world. An Argentinian bishop asked me, 'Why does the General Synod publish and promote reports before it finds out whether it agrees with them?' In the case of *Something to Celebrate* the Synod received it without enthusiasm, and only after it had first voted through a resolution strongly upholding the place of marriage, to make its position clear in case the report had led people to conclude otherwise.

In the dioceses we should look to similar streamlining, and the time must surely have come to change the nature of our Deanery Synods. I am convinced that we need effective deanery organizations, but I am not convinced that being a link in the synodical chain has drawn the best people together in our deaneries and given them the most relevant agendas. A deanery council strikes me as better sense – one that shares the task of the rural dean and is a place for reflection and planning about the life and mission of the churches and chaplaincies in an area.

Most of our dioceses seem to have three administrative centres: the diocesan office, the bishop's office and the cathedral. I cannot help wondering whether that is one administrative centre too many. Could the diocesan office and the bishop's office not be merged, for example? Could the cathedral, with its residentiary canons, be more fully involved as a service provider in the diocese? All too often one finds that the cathedral and the diocese are cohabitees rather than partners in a marriage.

I would argue that we can no longer afford to have almost every diocese maintaining full-time advisors and training staff for such things as evangelism, Sunday school teaching and social responsibility. We need to talk with the voluntary agencies such as CPAS, Church Army, Additional Curates Society and Scripture Union to see how much we could contract out. Such agencies may well have to rethink their styles of operation and we may need new agencies to emerge, but the principle of contracting out would slim down our central organizations. Again it seems crazy for every diocese to be reinventing certain wheels such as lay training and theological education. Several of our theological colleges have been producing correspondence and distance-learning courses which are of the highest quality and embody material that could be ideal for training readers, lay evangelists, lay pastoral workers and even clergy. We can no longer afford to go on living in separate worlds.

This brings us to the existence of our independent but officially recognized theological colleges. I hope that any present thinking towards replacing these colleges with one or two central national establishments will be abandoned. No idea could be more foolish. Quite apart from the fact that the Church would have to buy or build new buildings for any central establishments, the different theological schools add to the colour (literally and figuratively) and the operational morale of those who come through such bodies. There is a profound theological principle at issue here. God is a variety-loving God and his Spirit rarely blows where people plan for him to blow. Even in the New Testament era we can see this. The Jerusalem-based central structure of the first church was constantly having to rethink its strategy in the light of unplanned developments and maverick individuals like Philip the deacon, Stephen the martyr and St Paul. We must give the Holy Spirit as many places to touch down as possible!

I feel strongly that centralization is not the way to safeguard the future health of the Church. The history of the Church of England is packed with stories of individuals who started movements that changed the life of the Church at large far more than the decisions of any archbishop or synod. Centralization means that the Church is dependent on the perceptions and inspiration of a relatively small number of people. It would be strange to concentrate power and deci-sion-making at the centre at the very time when the national government is pursuing devolution. In voluntary organiza-tions motivation is related to involvement in decision-making. That does not mean that we do not need central structures, but it does mean that central structures should deal with central concerns, rather than trying to run the whole Church from the centre.

If one believes that God has providentially allowed the crises we are facing, then he is responsible for the situation where we are going to be increasingly short of stipendiary clergy. We have to ask what God's purpose for us must be in the future. One answer is that we need to deprofessionalize the clergy and train up what we cumbersomely call 'non-stipendiary clergy'. If we are to maintain anything near the present levels of eucharistic worship, then we need some sort of clergy to be available for this. Much of the present thinking about 'ordained local ministry' comes out of this mind-set. It may be the right mind-set, and I certainly believe in the value of non-stipendiaries, but I have my doubts.

Another way of looking at the clergy crisis is to ask whether God is calling the Church of England to become far more of a lay movement, with non-eucharistic worship becoming more prominent. One of the areas of unease that I discerned during my time in the Canterbury diocese was the under-use of readers. We had more readers – theologically trained lay ministers – in Canterbury than we had clergy. The trouble was that many of them felt they were under-used and under-valued. Our talk about ordained local ministry schemes only seemed to further disaffirm their ministry.

The thing that revolutionized my brother's rural ministry was the emergence of a team of readers who shared his ministry in his small group of congregations in the Cumbrian fells. I have a feeling that in some communities, many people will feel more accepting of ministry from a neighbour who is a reader than a neighbour who suddenly starts putting on a clerical collar on Sundays. And if that means, given our present ecclesial disciplines, that there are fewer Eucharists and more 'Services of the Word', it just might mean that we are nearer to where many of our parishioners find themselves.

There is, however, one aspect of a move towards lay-led churches and the development of the do-it-yourself worship culture that needs careful thought. There is the strong danger that a church run by lay activists will lose contact with its surrounding community. The traditional parish priest was, in fact, a bridging person between congregation and community. He led the congregation, but he also acted as the chaplain to the parish at large so that he or she was regarded as 'their vicar'. Losing a stipendiary clergy can mean the loss of that bridge and that chaplaincy. This is why some press for the concept of the ordained local person with great emphasis on the fact that the ideal candidate for such a post has recognition not only from the congregation, but also from the community. One or two of our rural benefices in Canterbury experimented with non-stipendiary 'village priests' to be the bridge people. Whatever answers are put in place to deal with this problem, it needs to be recognized that this is an issue that goes to the heart of our essential character as a Church. We are meant to be a Church for the people of England whether they come or not.

With all this said, however, I do not believe we have engaged with the real meaning of the Church as a lay movement. The essential ministry of a layperson is not inside buildings and wearing ministerial robes. The essential ministry is in the workplace, in recreational relationships, in the home and in wider society. In the past, Anglican laypeople have tended to see themselves as recipients of ministry rather than dispensers of it. They have seen Christianity as proper to their church buildings and their personal lives. This does not mean that there has been a lack of sincerity, but we do not seem to have had a strong sense of being apostolic people. I think that needs to change.

I remember being taken to Vespers in an ancient church in Rome where members of the Community of St Egidio gather each day. The service was lay-led and contained a simple sermon from a lay member. The church was packed with young adults, most of whom had come straight from their workplaces or colleges. It was a scene totally unlike anything I had found in Britain. The most impressive thing, however, was that the service was not what the community was about. It was for the community to gather, take stock and pray before going back into their lives in the everyday world conscious of who they were and whom they served.

After the service I had a meal with a couple of the members, young professionals, who told me of some of the projects that the community had mounted. I remember hearing about the establishment of hostels for immigrants and of key community members who travelled the world spending time in conciliation work in areas of conflict. In a strange way, for all its apparent clericalism, the Roman Catholic Church can teach a great deal about lay discipleship.

I think it was sad that the Church of England Men's Society closed down. Perhaps it had lost its way. Perhaps we need to break away from gender-specific lay groups, but I am convinced that we need to see the emergence of lay movements in the Church of England committed to the gospel and to serving the people of our country. At the moment it would seem that the Mothers' Union is the only lay movement of any size, and while some may feel its day is past, anyone who has seen the MU in African countries knows that the movement is capable of great things.

If the Church needs to think differently about its laity, I have an uncomfortable feeling that it also needs to think differently about its bishops. It has become increasingly clear in recent years that the way we operate episcopally is too expensive. It has been argued that the bishops are no charge on the parishes because their pay and expenses come from the Church Commissioners. This, however, as I mentioned earlier, means that money that might be available to subsidize the poorer parishes and dioceses is sucked into the maintenance of the present episcopal styles of operating. There is a marked difference in the pay and provision for a diocesan bishop and the pay and provision for a suffragan. I feel that the diocesans need to be phased back to something nearer the level of suffragans. I also feel that the differentials in pay and pensions between bishops and clergy should be, at the least, narrowed. As I look back on my time in office, I cannot avoid the feeling that we bishops were a somewhat pampered species, doing well when others in the Church were finding things difficult. When this sort of disparity is to be found, it does not help morale.

While bishops may need to live more modestly in the future, I feel they will have to operate in stronger and more authoritative ways. As those with responsibility for the provision of ministry within their diocese, I believe they must take a stronger role in decisions about selection, training and the deployment of their clergy. As leaders in mission, I believe they need to spend more time in their dioceses working at the strategic levels where they alone can operate in the name of Christ and his Church. At present some of our diocesans seem to spend a great deal of their time outside their dioceses on committees, liaison groups and working parties, which in themselves are evidence of the malady of an overbusy church. We need missionary bishops who stay in their diocese more, not to bury themselves as managers, but to be people who permeate the structures of society as ambassadors for the gospel cause and who stir up the cultural memory of Christ.

The 1998 Lambeth Conference called for bishops to see

themselves as primarily missionary bishops. This does not simply mean involvement in evangelistic missions – although that can be a powerful ministry. It means taking risky decisions to release and support new developments and ground-breaking initiatives. I found this sort of thing very difficult to do in so regulated and traditional a church. Church-planting in new areas often clashed with the parish system. Experimental congregations trying to work among the sorts of people who feel no affinity with the established liturgies of the Church need understanding bishops who will not throw canon law at them. Gifted laypeople who take initiatives and set up irregular ministries need help and support rather than coolness from the top. The temptation is always to play things by the book, even if we all know that this means a commitment to slow failure in a multi-cultural age. A church for the people of England has to find ways of starting where people are, and most people are not where the local vicar wants them to be.

Bishops need to be media people. They are uniquely positioned for this. I often felt it was tough on the other denominations who had outstanding people available, but a bishop is seen as 'Mr Christianity' by the media, and, in a world where much of the public discussion takes place on radio and television and in the press, we need our bishops to be available and to come across well.

Bishops also need disciplinary procedures that are workable, which has not been the case in the past. Whatever the values of freehold may be, and I can think of some, there simply has to be a way in which a priest who is dragging a church down can be moved or removed. No group of people is more important in the life of the Church than its clergy, but they exist to serve the Church and not to be served by it, and we simply cannot give everyone who wears a clerical collar job security for life and the right to ruin a worshipping community. If we believe that growth is important, we cannot sit by while shrinkage occurs.

Whether or not the suggestions I have been making are the best available, one thing remains clear. The Church of England will stand or fall in relation to the health or otherwise of its parish churches. It is true that the Church is more than the sum of its parishes. It is true that the great cathedrals have a remarkable ministry and there is evidence that more people are seeking them out for worship, but the parish churches are the foundations of the whole edifice. They are what defines whether the Church is truly of and for the people, or otherwise. If we were to make more energy available for the ministry of our parish churches, we could still use that energy in the wrong ways. I believe that, as things have become more difficult, we need to reaffirm the vision and the vocation of the Church of England.

We need to be congregations led by people who are committed to the vision of their church being there for the community as well as the congregation. There is no one way of doing this, because parishes and their communities vary enormously. The secret is that we have to blend an exclusive message with an inclusive manner. We have to keep relearning how to be unselfish, outgoing and welcoming as congregations, while still holding to our convictions about the will of God.

I remember talking with a young man from a Church of England congregation who was studying at Bible college. He wanted to spend his future life in Christian service. I asked him if he had considered ordination into the Church of England's ministry. 'The trouble is,' he said, 'that there are so many unconverted people in Church of England services that it spoils the worship!'

I have to admit that I felt unsympathetic to this point of view. 'Oh, what a pity,' I replied scornfully (may I be forgiven). 'You don't have to go out of church to find people to evangelize!' Over ten years after this conversation, I met up with that same young man and found that he was training for the ordained ministry. When I asked if our earlier conversation had played any part in this turn of events, he told me that he had forgotten the conversation. Ah well.

I think that it is the sign of a truly Christlike congregation if it can embrace both those who feel sure about their faith and those who are uncertain. I fear that there are many who are like that young man used to be, and who want their churches to be tailor-made for their own tastes in doctrine, worship and music. We have to identify this as selfishness and repent of it. One of the unhelpful dynamics of a congregation is that, like every organization of volunteers, it finds it difficult to organize for the tastes and preferences of those who are not its present members. This tends to militate against anyone joining who has not already joined! It therefore means that if a congregation has no children, young people or young adults within its present membership, it probably will never have them.

So how should today's parish churches go about their ministry? I think we can all learn by reflecting on the words of a successful football manager who was once asked for the secret of his team's success. His reply was, 'We do the simple things well.' I think that is also the secret for us. What, then, are the simple things? Here are my thoughts.

The first is, surely, to offer worship which can draw and nurture both the committed and the seeker, and which is in tune with the culture of the surrounding community. Success in this endeavour does not have to be limited to any one of the Church's traditions, nor does it mean the wholesale scrapping of a recognizably Anglican liturgy. I believe you can conduct worship in such a way that it can feel unstuffy and still have moments that are numinous and inspire silence and awe.

Linked to such worship there has to be effective preaching and teaching. Too many clergy and readers seem to have a low self-image about their abilities as preachers. The fact is that people do not dislike sermons. They dislike bad sermons! We need to realize afresh the great privilege of being spokes-people for God, and we need to speak out of a good knowledge of the world of the Bible and the world of our listeners. Those who listen to us need the opportunity to play back what they think they have heard and to make their own additions. Of course, the pulpit and the sermon are not the whole sum of a teaching ministry, but they are a far bigger part than is often realized.

The next simple thing, I suggest, is the recognition that the first responsibility of any generation of Christians is to help the next to discover the gospel. Anyone who has worked through the chapters of this book must know by now that I am convinced that passing on the faith to children is the most fundamental ministry of all. To do this we need to put energies into imaginative children's outreach and also help our members who have children at home to be able to explain their faith and build Christian homes.

Another simple thing is to love our community neighbours as ourselves, and to do so in practical ways. One of the most effective evangelizing churches I have ever seen was also one that buried itself in the social concerns of its needy parish, where the main source of employment, the local mine, had been closed. The church ran a used clothing shop and organized job retraining sessions. It was also packed on Sundays and I do not think that was a coincidence.

Loving one's neighbours and trying to heal their hurts can sometimes mean taking action against what brings those hurts. Those who minister in some of the deprived areas of our country have often found themselves pulled into what critics have called 'politics'. The truth is that they have only been pursuing the logic of love for their neighbour.

The final simple thing is the promotion of prayerfulness. This has to be demonstrated as much as taught, but the truest mark of belief in God is that we talk to him.

I believe that if a church does these five simple things well, then other things like youth work, evangelism and church growth will follow. In the case of many small congregations, however, I feel there is much to be gained by informal partnerships between congregations. It could well be that one congregation would not have the resources to mount a children's ministry or credible youth work, but that it could do so by pooling the resources it did have with another nearby church, or even two or three. Here we have to face the fact that the logical partners could be churches of other traditions or denominations. I have little patience for the complicated arrangements that churches are supposed to work through to become 'local ecumenical partnerships'. I find them, yet again, energy-sapping. I am, however, very sure that we must get on with working together with or without the ecclesiastical red tape.

This concern to be ever looking beyond the congregation to the wider community is what, for me, 'establishment' is all about. It also echoes the working of a God who 'became flesh and made his dwelling among us'. We are meant to be the

Church that is of, and for, the people of our country. If congregations of other denominations share this vision with us, that is all to the good. For us, however, we have no other legitimate option. It goes to the heart of our historic purpose and identity. And if, locally and nationally, we often appear to be more messy and haphazard than some would like, it is because we are more in touch with society than they realize. The truth is that society *is* messy and haphazard.

* * *

It was our annual schools' day in the cathedral – something that Judy Bainbridge and Rosemary Walters could be relied on to conduct with conspicuous success. It was my year to be the bishop who spoke to the children in the mini-service at the end of the day. The place was teeming with curious and excited children in their contrasting school uniforms. They were all sitting on the cathedral floor and I was up there in front in all my glad rags, mitre included. 'The children like a bishop to look like a bishop,' Judy had said.

I asked the children to look down, and then I asked them all to look up at the tall, slender pillars and arches and the great ceiling. Some of the children gasped at the sight.

'This place has been here for hundreds of years,' I said. 'And for all that time people have sat and stood where you are and said their prayers and thought about Jesus Christ. Isn't that an amazing thought?'

Canterbury Cathedral always brought that thought to me. It reminded me that the Christian faith has been part of our country for hundreds of years and that I am a Christian today because others passed that faith from one generation to another.

There was always a question, however, that came to mind as I looked around that historic place. How well were we, in our generation, passing on the good story of Jesus Christ? Would the cathedral, a century from now, still be a place where people prayed and worshipped, testifying to a faith that had stood the test of time?

I believe it will be so, but for that to happen the Church of England, alongside its sister Churches, will have to be brave and unselfish, to face changes and to take risks. Above all, it will have to be 'traditional' in the correct sense of the word, which does not mean hanging on desperately to some picture of a better past, but handing on winsomely the great story that can change the future.

And so the book is finished. I have tried to share my experience of keeping company with the Church of England in changing times. It is a Church I deeply love. It may have many weaknesses, but that is because it is a very human Church and there is strength as well as weakness in that humanity. I finish in that fine cathedral which is one of the great landmarks of Christianity in the nation and somehow symbolizes the mission of the Church of England, which is to keep the faith at the heart of national life. My prayer is that over the coming decades many people will come through those cathedral doors, and many more will be touched by the ministry of the clergy and congregations throughout the land. I hope that in some way or other millions will hear and respond to the song those children sang at my farewell: '*Turn your eyes upon Jesus . . .*'

Shapes of the Church to Come

by Bishop Michael Nazir-Ali

As a leading Bishop in the Church of England, Michael Nazir-Ali could justly be called a pillar of the establishment. But this book is a clear demonstration that even the pillars realise that the building could collapse if radical changes are not implemented soon – changes that will involve a serious re-evaluation of the church's mission and ministry in today's world.

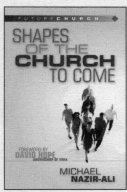

'This book provides thought-provoking insight on the most pressing issue facing the church today.'
Steve Chalke, Founding Director, Oasis Trust

'Bishop Michael Nazir-Ali explores some of the crucial questions facing the churches in the next decade…'
John Reardon, OBE
Former General Secretary of the Council of Churches for Britain and Ireland

'Rooted in Scripture and forged in pastoral practice, the key insights in this book address global and local issues that must not be ignored if the church is to stay alive and relevant.'
David Coffey, President, Baptist Union